WIDOR

Widor

The Life and Times of Charles-Marie Widor, 1844 – 1937

ANDREW THOMSON

OXFORD UNIVERSITY PRESS

1987

Oxford University Press, Walton Street, Oxford OX2 6DP

Oxford New York Toronto
Delhi Bombay Calcutta Madras Karachi
Petaling Jaya Singapore Hong Kong Tokyo
Nairobi Dar es Salaam Cape Town
Melbourne Auckland

and associated companies in
Beirut Berlin Ibadan Nicosia

Oxford is a trade mark of Oxford University Press

British Library Cataloguing in Publication Data

Thomson, Andrew
Widor: the life and times of
Charles-Marie Widor, 1844-1937.
1. Widor, Charles-Marie 2. Composers—
France—Biography
I. Title
780 '.92 '4 ML410.W64/
ISBN 0-19-316417-5

Library of Congress Cataloging-in-Publication Data

Thomson, Andrew, 1944-
Widor: the life and times of Charles-Marie Widor,
1844-1937.
Bibliography: p. 109
Includes index.
1. Widor, Charles Marie, 1844-1937. 2. Composers—
France—Biography. I. Title.
ML410.W64T5 1987 780 '.92 '4 [B] 87-15176
ISBN 0-19-316417-5

Set by Downdell Ltd., Abingdon, Oxon.
Printed and bound in
Great Britain by Biddles Ltd.
Guildford and King's Lynn

for my wife Susan

FOREWORD

IN 1933, when I was nineteen, I sat beside Widor on the organ bench during a Sunday Mass at Saint-Sulpice. He was then eighty-nine. I have two memories of that brief encounter: just how the Adagio of his *Suite Latine* should be played, and asking him to autograph my copy of his Symphonie No. 5, now a prized memento. I would never have thought of asking him when he wrote it. Nor, apparently, did any of his compatriots.

He was, of course, already a living *monument historique* in 1914, when, at the age of seventy, he became Permanent Secretary of the *Académie*. The astonishing thing is that no one in France or abroad ever wrote a book about him. In vain I hunted Paris for one. Nor, in his native city of Lyons, could I find even the briefest of monographs or a short *plaquette* commemorating him. More serious, perhaps, was the lack of any exact dating of the earlier *Symphonies pour Orgue* in any reference book, although Widor himself could have been consulted at any time during the last fifty years of his long life. Alas, like his famous 'Toccata', Widor was taken for granted. Far younger composers than him have lived to see a decline of interest in their work as they grew older. Widor, himself a junior Parisian contemporary of Rossini, Liszt, Berlioz, Franck, and Saint-Saëns, survived into the world of Dupré, Duruflé, and Messiaen, composers of organ music in an age that evidently thought Widor's hardly worth investigating.

But Charles-Marie Widor was far more than just the composer of what is arguably the most famous organ toccata since Bach. He was undeniably what the French themselves would term *un monsieur*, and Mr Thomson's book, the first on him to appear anywhere in Europe, does more than fill a gap on the shelves of a music library. Beginning with the documented determination of the correct year of Widor's birth, he supplies an engrossing account of the musical, social, religious, and political background against which Widor lived his life. Coinciding with a renewed interest in Widor's pioneering, 'symphonic' organ music, the following pages should prove fascinating to a far wider circle than that which encloses the organ world.

Felix Aprahamian

ACKNOWLEDGEMENTS

THIS biography of Charles-Marie Widor could not have been written without the support of two people. It was Jerrold Northrop Moore who first suggested that I undertake it, and with great generosity of time and effort he has watched over and guided my work in progress, giving me the full benefit of his experience as a biographer of Elgar, and much necessary criticism. Felix Aprahamian was so kind as to put his personal library at my disposal, and I also gained much from his vast and intimate knowledge of French music and civilization. To both these friends I owe more than I can properly express here. I alone, however, bear the responsibility for the ideas and opinions expressed in these pages.

I have also been fortunate in receiving magnificent assistance from other sources. I would like to express my gratitude to the following: M. François Lesure and the staff of the Bibliothèque Nationale; M. Emmanuel Bondeville, Secrétaire perpétuel de l'Académie des Beaux-Arts; Mme Françoise Dumas and staff of the Institut de France; M. l'Abbé Pierre Ploix of La Maison Diocésaine de Paris; M. le Vicaire de l'Eglise de Saint-Sulpice; the librarians of the Conservatoires of Paris and Brussels; Mrs Sheila Bellaigue of the Royal Archives, Windsor Castle; the Headmaster and Archivist of Hurstpierpoint College; Miss Jutta Avaly of United Music Publishers Ltd; Mr Arthur Searle of the Royal Philharmonic Society; Mr Michael Anderson of the Reid Music Library, Edinburgh University; the staff of the Archives Nationales de France, the Mairies of Lyon and Annonay, the British Library, the Académie de Lyon, the BBC Music Library, the University of Sussex library, and the Biblioteca Municipal do Porto.

I am indebted to the following for writing to me with their reminiscences or with other information: Mme Marie-Claire Alain, Mme Jacqueline Englert-Marchal, the late Mme Yvonne Lefébure, Mme Maurice Duruflé, Mme Alice-Charles Tournemire, M. Jean Langlais, M. Charles Jaillet, Mrs Ann Bastow, Mrs Ann Maddocks, Dr Roger Nichols, Dr Michael de

Cossart, Dr W. G. Ibberson, Dr G. L. Barnard, and Mr Rodolphe d'Erlanger.

Only after I had completed the typescript and sent it to the publisher did I learn of the existence of John Richard Near's doctoral thesis 'The Life and Work of Charles-Marie Widor' (University of Boston, 1985). His catalogue of Widor's compositions is invaluable, and it is with gratitude that I have referred to it.

Finally, I must not forget the interest in my work shown by my friends David M. Patrick and Nicholas Dicker, who kept me liberally supplied with scores, records, and tapes. And last, but by no means least, the moral—and indeed financial—support of my wife Susan, my mother, and relatives. They have provided the tools for me to finish the job.

Andrew Thomson
Clevedon 1986

CONTENTS

LIST OF PLATES

INTRODUCTION

AT the centre of French organ music in the nineteenth century stands the work of the organ builder Aristide Cavaillé-Coll (1811-99). His extraordinary combination of mechanical genius and artistic vision made possible the achievements of César Franck, Charles-Marie Widor, and their school.

Descended from a family of organ builders in Toulouse, Cavaillé-Coll was befriended by Rossini, who recognized his gifts and persuaded him to move to Paris.[1] There he made his name by winning a Government-sponsored competition to rebuild the Clicquot-Lefèvre organ in the Abbaye de Saint-Denis, which he completed in 1841. At a time when France was making outstanding contributions to scientific development, he brought his formidable knowledge of mathematics and physics to bear on organ building. But, in contrast to contemporaries like the physiologist Claude Bernard and the biologist Louis Pasteur—who were unable to reconcile their simultaneous beliefs in science and religion[2]—Cavaillé-Coll possessed a uniquely integrated vision. A deeply religious man, he found no philosophical contradiction in placing science at the service of the Catholic church, and this despite the Encyclical and Syllabus of 1864 promulgated by Pope Pius IX which denied that 'the Roman Pontiff can and ought to reconcile himself and reach agreement with progress, liberalism and modern civilisation'.[3]

Cavaillé-Coll began his career in an artistic vacuum. The tradition of organ music and performance in France had been severely weakened as a result of the Revolution of 1789. Even after the Restoration of the Monarchy in 1814, it remained in a state of decadence, insulated from the Classical and Romantic movements and from the rediscovery of J. S. Bach which was sweeping the rest of Northern Europe. The first publication of Bach's organ works by Peters (1845-7) created scarcely a ripple of interest among French players. Two exceptions proved the rule: the unappreciated Alexandre Boëly, organist of Saint-Germain-l'Auxerrois, and the recluse Charles Valentin Alkan (using a pedal-piano at Erard's studio).[4]

The general musical and technical limitations of French organists were scathingly dismissed by François Fétis, Director of the Brussels Conservatoire: 'Not one of them has what may be called an organist's training. Not one of them could master the great compositions of Bach.'[5] For this state of affairs, the condition of the instruments was to be blamed, rather than the teaching of the worthy Organ Professor at the Paris Conservatoire, François Benoist, whose task was made the more difficult and discouraging thereby; perhaps not surprisingly, his best students—Alkan, Lefébure-Wély, Franck, and Saint-Saëns—were also excellent pianists. Their efforts were vitiated by such factors as decaying eighteenth-century organs, unsteady wind-pressures, and unstandardized pedal-boards.[6]

Cavaillé-Coll was not slow to realize that if organ music was to be regenerated in an age of science, it must be achieved by an instrument of unprecedented scale and power, approaching—or even in some ways matching—the orchestra of Berlioz. Cavaillé-Coll's innovations made use of the most advanced technology of his time. Steady wind-pressures in ample quantities provided his new instruments with increased sustaining power. He incorporated the pneumatic Barker lever permitting manual couplings hitherto impractical on account of the heavy action which they produced. By means of the ventil pedal mechanism, stops could be prepared in advance and brought into play on the instant. Swell enclosures provided increased dynamic expression, keyboards and pedal-boards were extended, and reed and string stops were voiced to match orchestral sonorities.

Only gradually did the organists grasp the full aesthetic implications of these developments: the flamboyant *titulaires* of fashionable churches were content to indulge the hedonistic tastes of the *nouveaux riches* with improvisations based on little substance other than crude pictorialism and extreme contrasts of colour and dynamics. The striking new features of Cavaillé-Coll's instruments were open to abuse: Widor himself retailed an account of the inauguration of Cavaillé-Coll's organ at the Madeleine in 1846: 'Three Improvisations by M. Fessy, organist of the parish, and three Improvisations by M. Lefébure-Wély, organist of Saint-Roch. Two hours of unbearable chatter. Imitations of the sounds of nature were in fashion: "M. X", wrote a critic, "inflicted a thunderstorm on us, which he mistakenly failed to announce with any strokes of genius." ' [7]

A turning-point in the history of the French organ was a recital given in 1852 on the new Cavaillé-Coll instrument at Saint-Vincent-de-Paul by Nicolas Lemmens. This great Belgian organist claimed an impressive pedigree of teachers: the line stemmed from J. S. Bach through his son C. P. E. Bach, his pupil Johann Forkel, his pupil Johann Rinck, and thence to Lemmens's own teacher Adolf Hesse.[8] There was passed down from hand to hand not only manuscript copies of Bach's works, but also a tradition of performance purportedly authentic.

On this occasion, Lemmens's legato playing and pedal technique which he brought to his interpretations of Bach amazed the distinguished audience—which included Gounod, Ambroise Thomas, Benoist, Alkan and Franck. Afterwards, Benoist wrote to Cavaillé-Coll: 'What struck me above all was the calm religious grandeur and that severity of style so befitting the majesty of the temple of God. In these times, it is of great merit, in my eyes, to remain faithful to the traditions of the great masters who, in the last century, have laid the foundations of the true art of the organ.' [9]

For Cavaillé-Coll above all, Lemmens's recital 'was the light'.[10] At last there had appeared the organist who could understand and exploit his instruments, and in turn be enhanced by them. The organ builder took a decision which shows the quality of the man: he himself would create a new French school of players. Fortified by Benoist's generous admission, Cavaillé-Coll founded what amounted to private and informal scholarships at his own expense to send promising students to study with Lemmens, who was now Organ Professor at the Brussels Conservatoire under Fétis. As a result, from 1855, Clement Loret, Alphonse Mailly, and Alexandre Guilmant received Lemmens's instruction. This great teacher was to publish his method in 1862 as his *Ecole d'orgue*.[11]

Meanwhile, the seed sown by Lemmens had found some patches of fertile ground in Paris itself. In 1857, Saint-Saëns was appointed to the Madeleine, and Franck to Sainte-Clotilde the following year; the battle for a higher artistic conception of church music had begun. And Cavaillé-Coll, with renewed hope and confidence went on to build his finest organs: for

Saint-Sulpice (1862) and Notre Dame (1868), as well as for a number of newly erected churches—notably Sainte-Clotilde (1858) and the Trinité (1869)—which took their place amid Baron Haussmann's reconstruction of Paris during the Second Empire of Napoleon III.

1

WIDOR'S FORMATIVE YEARS

CHARLES-MARIE-JEAN-ALBERT WIDOR was born in Lyon at 19 rue Sala on 21 February 1844 'à deux heures du soir', as his birth certificate curiously words it.[1] It is fortunate that the document exists, for the date of Widor's birth was often stated as 22 February 1845. He himself thought that was the case, as he wrote on his note of admission to the Institut de France in 1910.

His origins were Hungarian on his father's side, although his forebears had been settled in Alsace for a century. Of these, his great-grandfather commanded the Brigade of Sambre-et-Meuse while Widor's grandfather settled in Rouffac near Colmar as an organ builder.[2] The trade was carried on by Widor's father, François Charles (aged 33 at his son's birth) who was an organist of considerable ability in his own right.

On a visit to Lyon to demonstrate one of the family's instruments, François took the decision to remain there. He became organist of Saint-François and married.[3] Perhaps he aspired higher, for in the year of Charles-Marie's birth, the *Gazette musicale* reported that 'This autumn of 1844, a young man from Lyon, but of Hungarian origin, came to Paris to make a first appearance: he was Charles Widor, composer, pianist and organist. He returned at once to Lyon where he had a numerous following.'[4] His reputation even reached the ears of Cavaillé-Coll, who, in 1857, wrote to the Treasurer of Sainte-Madeleine, Tareu about the dedication of its new organ: 'We know M. Widor . . . who is both extremely talented as a musician and possesses extensive knowledge of the theory and practice of organ building: his judgment would be that of a well-informed expert, and would be sufficient guarantee for the Council'.[5]

François's wife, Françoise Elisabeth Peiron (known as 'Fanny') was of a family which had been firmly settled in Annonay since the sixteenth century, although believed to be of Italian origin. The Widors were proud of their family connections. François

Charles was the cousin of Claude Bourget, grandfather of the celebrated critic and writer Paul Bourget.[6] Fanny was very distantly related to the great scientific Montgolfier family who had established themselves at Annonay in 1693 as paper manufacturers;[7] in June 1783, the brothers Etienne and Joseph flew the first hot-air balloon. The Montgolfiers were themselves descended from the Duret family, into which Fanny's great-great-great-grandfather had married in 1647.[8]

The Montgolfiers were among the pioneers of the scientific and industrial revolution which gathered increasing momentum during the course of the nineteenth century, and the young Charles-Marie was to witness the resulting social upheavals. His birthplace Lyon—a large silk-manufacturing city at the junction of the Rhone and the Saône—was described by Charles Dickens (passing through *en route* for Italy in the very year of the organist's birth): 'All the little streets whose name is Legion, were scorching, blistering and sweltering: the houses, high and vast, dirty to excess, rotten as old cheeses and as thickly peopled.'[9] During the next decade, however, these old buildings were to be swept away in a monumental scheme of town planning that was part of Napoleon III's programme of public works.

Lyon, with its Cathedral, opera-house, and concert society, boasted a flourishing cultural life. Both Charles-Marie and his brother Paul received an excellent general education at the Lycée de Lyon. The former became a brilliant scholar in Latin and Greek[10] and a keen amateur painter[11]—an interest which was to stand him in good stead in the future. His father took charge of his musical education: his organ-playing advanced so rapidly that, at the age of eleven, he was made organist of his school chapel. He also deputized for his father at Saint-François[12] on its Cavaillé-Coll organ, described as a 'Grand Orgue de 32 pieds'.[13] Paul Widor likewise inherited musical gifts as an organist. For his living, however, he took to the Law, becoming Chief Clerk to the Lyon Court of Appeal.[14]

Charles-Marie's career was settled one memorable day in 1858, as he recounted to Marcel Dupré:

We lived opposite the church . . . and it was a special occasion when M. Cavaillé-Coll, passing through Lyon, was the guest of my parents. I was fourteen years old when, one day at table, he pronounced: 'When Charles-Marie has finished his studies, he must go to study in Brussels with the great organist Lemmens, to whom I shall introduce him. I have already sent young Guilmant from Boulogne-sur-Mer to him, who is gifted to the extent of being able to read a work of Bach with hands and feet together.' Such was the art of the organist in 1858.[15]

After young Widor passed his Baccalauréat in Classics, Cavaillé-Coll's plan was set in motion. As a French national, he was not eligible to enrol at the Brussels Conservatoire, but Lemmens agreed to accept him as a private pupil. A hard apprenticeship was in store, which lasted for four years.[16] All Widor saw of the city was the park, which he had to cross each day: 'Every morning, at 8.00 a.m., an organ lesson with Lemmens during which I had to play a new piece by Bach or some other Classical composer. Eight hours a day had to suffice.'
Stringent criticism was forthcoming.

In the madness of youth, speed is the goal for a virtuoso; when I thought· I had succeeded impeccably [with Bach's Fugue in D major, BWV 532] I had profoundly deceived myself. 'That is empty', said Lemmens, 'mechanical, without will.' What did he mean by will? I didn't dare to ask. However, I finally understood: it is the art of the orator, his authority which is imposed by calm, order and the just proportions of discourse. For musicians, the will is manifest above all in rhythm. A mechanical piano does not hold our interest for any longer than the tic-toc of a clock, one doesn't listen to it; whereas the mastery of a Liszt or a Rubinstein *who did not play fast*, has moved the world.[17]

Widor also studied composition privately with Fétis, the Director of the Brussels Conservatoire, described by Wagner as 'this autocratically posturing man.'[18] As well as being a prolific composer of symphonies, operas, and masses, he was a man of an encyclopaedic musical culture, his achievements embracing a *Histoire général de la musique* and the *Biographie universelle des musiciens* which testifies to his vast network of personal contacts throughout Europe.

After he had finished his organ practice, Widor spent 'about two hours every evening at his table with written work, for an entire fugue had to be brought to Fétis each week'. During these lessons, Fétis 'often spoke of Rinck, whom he had visited, of Kittel, his musical father, and of their great common ancestor, Sebastian Bach'.[19]

From Fétis, Widor received a thorough training in the basic principles and inner dynamics of composition, as exemplified by the works of Bach, Handel, Haydn, Mozart, and Beethoven, the art of thematic combination and development, and the balancing and contrasting of keys. These streams of musical thought, Fétis warned, were all too easily muddied by the frenzy and subjective expression of Romanticism and the predominantly operatic culture of France and the Latin countries.

However, this extended course of private tuition placed Widor in a state of isolation far removed from the institutional life of a conservatoire or university with its student camaraderie and competition. No ceremony marked the termination of his studies. Henceforth, he would have to make his own way in the musical world, without any diplomas or prizes behind him, relying solely on his talents and the support of private patrons in the face of the hostility shown to him by many products of the great conservatoires.

2

OPPORTUNITIES BECKON

AT the conclusion of these studies in Brussels, Widor returned to Lyon to take over the position of organist of Saint-François from his father, who was doubtless proud to give way to his gifted son, described by the *Biographie universelle des musiciens* in the following terms: 'His talent was as remarkable as it was precocious, and his reputation soon outstripped the limits of the town.'[1] Cavaillé-Coll lost no time in promoting his young protégé, frequently summoning him to Paris and other parts of France and abroad to assist in the proving and testing of his new organs. For this purpose, the organ builder employed not only the pupils of Lemmens, but also the best products of Benoist's class—Lefébure-Wély, Franck, Saint-Saëns, and Chauvet. The composite recitals which were given on these occasions brought Widor into valuable contact with them: at this level, there was no manifestation of the petty jealousies which he was frequently to encounter from lesser men.

Saint-Saëns represented a model of what Widor himself aimed to become: an urbane man of *métier*, versatile composer in all forms of music, brilliant pianist and organist, well travelled, and vastly cultivated. Yet Widor was sufficiently mature to recognize the essential greatness of Franck, albeit masked by his dowdy personal appearance and relative lack of general education and social polish; his spiritual qualities shone through his *Six Pièces pour Grand Orgue*, Op. 16 (1860-2) and comparatively austere improvisations.

In 1866, Cavaillé-Coll moved from the rue Vaugiraud to new manufacturing premises in the Avenue du Maine, a former ballroom with excellent acoustics. There Widor had the opportunity to meet the élite of the musical and scientific communities: Rossini, Liszt, Gounod, Ambroise Thomas, and the distinguished physicists and acousticians Helmholtz, Foucault, and Lissajous. The new recruit must have made a most favourable impression, for he was to receive much encouragement from them; indeed, we are told that the veteran Rossini 'took a liking to him'.[2] Widor also took part in the concerts held in the Avenue du Maine together with his brother Paul, a singer as well as an organist; some of the other regular artists were to play an important role in his musical life: Marsick and Delsart for whom he wrote concertos for violin and cello respectively, and the amateur singers Marie Trélat and Henriette Fuchs.[3]

It was to the influence of Saint-Saëns that Widor owed his first major engagement. In September 1865 he attended the International Exhibition of Oporto as organist of the specially erected Crystal Palace, an iron-and-glass structure modelled on Paxton's famous 1851 original in London. The British influence—reflecting the commercial links with Portugal forged by the Treaty of Methuen in 1703—extended even to the organ erected in the Palace. It had been built by J. W. Walker, and previously exhibited at the London Exhibition of 1862; it was a considerable instrument of three manuals and pedals.

Arriving only three days before the opening ceremony, Widor rapidly composed a special *Grande Phantasia* for organ and orchestra which was performed under the baton of the Portuguese pianist Arthur Napoleão. This earned its composer the decoration of Commander of the Order of Christ of Portugal from the hand of King Luis I. Widor also played the organ for the Mass celebrated by the Polish priest Carlos Mikoszewsky at Saint-Bento-da-Victoria; appropriately, it was brought to a close with the Polish National Anthem, a striking gesture towards the people whose native land had been partitioned between Prussia, Austria, and Russia. It was a situation to touch Widor's Hungarian inheritance.

In a lighter vein, he took a leading part in the series of popular concerts—complete with raffles—held in the Crystal Palace, and attended by 'crowds of listeners in the large central hall and galleries . . . a brilliant festival worthy of the artists who appeared, by popular acclaim . . . in addition to the musical attractions, there were the splendours of abundant lighting'.

The programmes featured a number of operatic fantasias, a genre very popular in the nineteenth century. In Perni's Trios on themes from *Rigoletto* and *I Puritàni*, Napoleão and the cellist Casella were joined by Carlos Widor (*sic!*) at the harmonium. For a *Duet on a theme from Belisario* and *Homage to the Crystal*

Palace, Widor became part of a two-piano team with Napoleão. He himself contributed a Serenade for quintet—specially composed for the Popular Concerts—and a Trio. Each concert usually began and ended with an organ solo: a Concerto by Handel, a Concerto (*sic*) by Mendelssohn, Mozart's *Turkish March*, Meyerbeer's March from *Le Prophète*. But of particular interest is the inclusion of some of Widor's own organ pieces: a Sonata, Phantasia, March, and Final, all otherwise unspecified.[4]

It is highly probable that these were early versions of movements later to be included in the set of organ symphonies which Widor published in 1872 as his Op. 13.[5] The following account by his pupil Marcel Dupré provides evidence of at least some composition during the lifetime of Rossini (who died on 13 November 1868):

M. Cavaillé-Coll . . . found the works of the young maître a little harsh. 'I must take you to Rossini,' he said to him, 'he will certainly have the same impression as me.' Widor had to comply one day, and play the *Final* of his *Symphonie No. 2* for organ on a miserable upright piano. Helpfully, Rossini undertook the pedal part, then turned to Cavaillé-Coll: 'Of course not, this piece is very interesting and pleases me. Go on, young man!'[6]

The dating of the symphonies is problematic, for no manuscript sources are known. The evidence suggests that the Op. 13 symphonies are in fact suites of movements originally written separately for use in services and recitals. Moreover, it is possible that certain movements at least may have evolved over a period of up to 12 years—especially after Widor became organist of Saint-Sulpice in 1870. And the process of revision went on, as evidenced in revised editions of both sets of symphonies, Op. 13 (Nos. 1-4) and Op. 42 (Nos. 5-8) in 1900-1, and again during the period 1914-18 and 1920. The critic Hugues Imbert, a friend of Widor, revealed that he 'conceived a work rapidly, always mistrusting his facility, and regretting in principle that he had delivered to the publisher pages which would have gained from ripening'.[7]

The Op. 13 symphonies contain an almost bewildering variety of styles—Baroque, Classical, and Romantic—which testify to Widor's wide and comprehensive knowledge of music and powers of absorption. The resulting eclecticism is a feature of the art, architecture, and music of the Second Empire. Meyerbeer—its presiding composer of operas—had also received a formal

Germanic training in Berlin before being overwhelmed by the experience of Rossini's operas in Italy. Contact with Rossini may well have helped Widor to lighten his style and develop his marked gift of melody.

Each of these symphonies includes serious movements of fully worked-out Baroque contrapuntal and fugal writing, reflecting the strict disciplines of Fétis, as well as the organ works of Mendelssohn and Boëly which Widor admired.[8] The 'Prélude' (No. 1), 'Fugue' (No. 1), and 'Praeludium Circulare' (No. 2) are patently the work of a young composer in their complexity and fierce angularity of part-writing. Maturity, however, is reached with the magnificent 'Prélude' (No. 3), a tripartite structure with quasi-fugal invention over powerful pedal-points. The constantly modulating style in heavy Baroque sequences achieves a plasticity of form and a truly aspiring 'Gothic' character. The fantasia-style 'Salve Regina' (No. 2) is based on plainchant—the sole example of its use in Widor's organ music before the final 'Gothique' and 'Romane' symphonies. The 'Toccata' (No. 4) consists of a majestic French Overture with heavily dotted Lullian rhythms. The contrasting 'Fugue' is smooth and mellifluous.

The fashionable but tepid atmosphere of the salon hangs over many of the slow movements. Of these, the best includes the serene Adagio (No. 3), a canon at the octave over pedal-points. In the Andante cantabile (No. 4), a naïve folk-type melody—with echoes of Beethoven's 'Pathétique' Sonata—recurs three times with varied accompaniment. The melody of the Adagio (No. 4), with its gentle syncopations, evokes the sentimental atmosphere of Mendelssohn's *Songs without Words*.

Two march movements of ceremonial splendour find their prototypes in Meyerbeer's operas. The popular 'March Pontificale' (No. 1) is crudely effective with its main theme in massive chords. The less well-known 'Marcia' (No. 3) is a magnificent piece of sustained invention, the melodic impulse continuing in an unbroken flow throughout. In lighter vein, the 'Pastorale' (No. 2) has great charm in its lilting, syncopated rhythms and haunting refrain. The spirit of Mendelssohn's *Midsummer Night's Dream* pervades the 'Scherzo' (No. 4) with its moto perpetuo staccato semiquavers. In the middle section a new theme is treated in canon at the octave.

Two of the symphonies end with brilliant showpieces. The 'Final' (No. 2) is a moto perpetuo—a dazzling flow of quavers interrupted periodically by grand rhetorical cadences worthy of Handel. The rumbustuous rondo theme of the 'Final' (No. 4) is in itself a somewhat commonplace idea but raised to a higher level of inspiration by its development. But the 'Final' (No. 3) can claim perhaps to be the outstanding movement of the entire set. In its manual writing and striking harmonic progressions, it shows the clear influence of Liszt. The disturbing, turbulent character of this music is created by the furious activity of broken-chord figuration over slow rates of harmonic change.

Although the origins of many of these movements were mundane, it is nevertheless instructive to view them in comparison with the general level of organ music in this period, typified by the crude imitations of nature in Lemmens's *The Storm*, and the blatant valse rhythms of Lefébure-Wély's *Sorties* which were played to the ecclesiastical gallery with the full encouragement of the clergy.[9]

The enormous breadth of scale of the movements from Widor's symphonies, achieved by wide-ranging tonal relationships—at times modulating to the extreme limit of the tonal compass— goes some considerable way to justifying the grandiose and original appellation 'Symphonie pour Grand Orgue' in the Op. 13 set; doubtless, Widor was also tempted by the quasi-orchestral voicing of stops and sonic combinations so characteristic of Cavaillé-Coll's instruments. He had some precedents in Alkan's 'Symphonie for Piano Solo' (part of the *Etudes*, Op. 39 of 1857, dedicated to Fétis[10]) and Franck's 'Grande pièce symphonique' (from the *Six Pièces*, 1860-1, dedicated to Alkan).

This period also produced the Symphonie No. 1 in F, Op. 16, for orchestra, published 1873. This is a unified work for Mozartian forces in the standard four movements, and is a considerable achievement for a young Frenchman lacking a solid symphonic tradition in his own country. The influences of Beethoven, Mendelssohn, and Schumann are apparent, but well integrated. No very individual voice makes itself heard, but there is terseness of argument, rhythmic vitality, and melodic charm. Still more remarkable is the totally assured handling of the orchestra, which is pungent, incisive, and clear.

During these years a visit to Rome made a profound and lasting impression on Widor, whose interest in classical civilization remained with him for the rest of his life. The sight of the speakers' rostrum in the Forum produced this observation:

It was there that the heart of the world beat for centuries; and I imagined huge crowds acclaiming Cicero or Caesar. I had not reflected that the orator's voice does not carry far in the open air, and that to have an effect on the public, it must be contained within appropriate limits. The place is constricted, barely accommodating 300 or 400 listeners; it was all that was necessary for the Idea to put forth its wings and fly from there to the ends of the Empire.[11]

The massive Coliseum likewise stimulated his imagination. Henceforth the organ—with its 'sustaining tones which seem to have neither beginning nor end'—evoked in his mind these timeless remains of antiquity: 'In its presence, let us call to mind the monumental constructions of the past, let us bow down in reverence and imagine that we are going to move to song the Egyptian pyramid or Roman Coliseum.'[12] Returning to his own century, he may well have been inspired to write the 'March Pontificale' by the sight of Pope Pius IX—author of the doctrine of Papal Infallibility (1870)—being carried in triumphant procession.

In Paris Widor began to enlarge his circle of social acquaintances in high places. A close friendship with the banker Baron Emile d'Erlanger began in 1867 when he gave the opening recital on the Cavaillé-Coll chamber organ which the Baron had installed in his music room at 20 rue Taitbout. On this instrument, Widor tells us that he 'registered, with Rossini, the *Offertoire* of his [*Petit messe solemnelle*] in the presence of Cavaillé-Coll'.[13]

Emile d'Erlanger, born in Frankfurt, was a great lover of the arts and a good amateur violinist who played chamber music every evening after dinner. To him Widor dedicated his Trio in B♭, Op. 19 for violin, cello, and piano (1874), a work of a broad melodic character, reflecting the influence of early Beethoven. Of Emile's three sons, Baron Frédéric became a minor composer of operas, at first under the name of Frédéric Regnal.

The cultivated banker—who counted the Empress Eugénie among his acquaintances—played a major part in the social, artistic, and political life of the Second Empire, and brought Widor into the *beau monde*. Emile had supported the Princesse de

Metternich in mounting the ill-fated performances of *Tannhäuser* at the Paris Opéra in 1861: Wagner himself 'found him at all times a true friend as concerned for my well-being as for the success of my undertaking'.[14] On the political level, dealings of a rather murkier nature were made with the cunning Prefect of the Seine, Baron Haussmann, whose rebuilding of Paris was financed by an un-paralleled mortgaging of the city.[15]

In 1868, Widor took part in a musical event of outstanding national importance—the inauguration of the new organ of Notre Dame de Paris. The restoration of the cathedral by the leading authority on medieval architecture, Viollet-le-Duc, had been followed by the rebuilding of the Clicquot organ, a task entrusted to Cavaillé-Coll. In February the official Commission—which included Rossini, Auber, Thomas, Benoist, Lemmens, Duc, and Lissajous—subjected the new instrument of 86 stops and five manuals to a thorough examination before pronouncing it to be 'of the first order'.

The opening recital took place on 6 March in the presence of Mgr. Darboy, Archbishop of Paris. No less than seven organists in turn displayed the organ's resources. Of these, Loret per-formed Bach's Prelude and Fugue in E minor, BWV 548; Saint-Saëns, the 'March' from his own cantata *Prométhée*; Franck, his 'Fantasie in C'; and Guilmant his 'March Funèbre' and 'Chant Séraphique'. Widor—still 'organiste à Lyon'—concluded the pro-gramme with an improvisation designed to demonstrate the range and variety of its registers.[16] However, this instrument, perhaps the most magnificent example of Cavaillé-Coll's handiwork, was entirely wasted on the perfunctory and unimaginative *titulaire* Sergent; only on very rare occasions—such as the recital by Anton Bruckner in 1869—was it heard to full advantage before 1900 when Louis Vierne became organist.

An era was drawing to a close. Rossini died in 1868, and the following year Berlioz joined him in the grave; the latter's funeral at the Trinité was attended by Widor.[17] A few days later, on 16 March 1869, he returned there for the opening recital on Cavaillé-Coll's new organ (at which, from 1871, Guilmant was to preside), together with the *titulaire* Chauvet, Saint-Saëns, and Franck. Widor, who played his own 'Andante' and 'Scherzo' 'with very great technical skill', was deeply moved by Franck's improvisation on this occasion: 'The themes, the development, the formal completeness are all equally to be admired: in fact, he has never written down any better music than he played today.' [18]

Widor's star continued to rise. In 1869, he became assistant to Saint-Saëns at the Madeleine.[19] Very soon afterwards, he was to be engulfed in the catastrophe which overwhelmed France; yet at the same time, he achieved one of his greatest prizes.

3

SAINT-SULPICE

ON 31 December 1869, while Widor was playing for the Mass at the Madeleine, news came that Lefébure-Wély, the organist of Saint-Sulpice, had died.[1] On the recommendation of Gounod and Cavaillé-Coll, Widor was immediately appointed as acting organist in his place.[2] The official position is that he became *titulaire* on 13 January 1870.[3] Widor's own story was rather different. According to this, his initial appointment scandalized a number of Paris organists—doubtlessly because he was very young and had not been a student at the Paris Conservatoire—and a joint letter of protest was sent to the Curé, the Abbé Hamon. The latter cautiously imposed a one-year probationary period to run from 1 January 1870. On its expiry, no decision was forthcoming, and Widor deemed it more prudent not to raise the matter.[4] Thus it came about that he remained acting organist for 64 years—a reign to equal that of Queen Victoria!

The parish church of Saint-Sulpice—described by Edward Gibbon as 'one of the noblest structures in Paris'[5]—is of a truly Baroque grandeur. Its foundation stone was laid in 1646 by Anne of Austria, Queen of Louis XIII. The nave preserves the traditional form of a Latin cross, lined with arcades of Roman arches and Corinthian pillars beneath a vaulted roof. The imposing west end façade was designed by Servandoni with two asymmetrical towers.

A distinctive feature of Saint-Sulpice was its combination of parish church and seminary for the training of priests, the latter founded by Jean-Jacques Olier, (Curé, 1642-52). Its best-known product was the controversial Ernest Renan, author of *La Vie de Jésus*.[6]

After the upheavals of the Revolution of 1789, in which the church was turned into a Temple of Victory, a revival of Catholicism followed the Restoration of the Monarchy in 1814. The Abbé Hamon (Curé, 1851-74)—a man of Ultramontane

principles, believing in the absolute supremacy and infallibility of
the Pope—was greatly concerned with the artistic contribution to
the worship of God. In 1855, he reorganized the choir, which
now consisted of a choirmaster, 24 boys, 10 men, and two players
of serpents or double-basses. (In accordance with the usual
practice in French churches, the choir has its own 'Petit Orgue'
and organist.) The celebrated murals in the Chapelle des
Anges—'Heliodorus driven from the Temple' and 'Jacob
wrestling with the Angel'—were commissioned from Eugène
Delacroix in 1862.[7] In the same year, the rebuilding of
Clicquot's 1781 'Grand Orgue' in the west gallery was completed by Cavaillé-Coll, retaining Chalgrin's Grecian case adorned
with Clodion's sculptured figures. The new and huge five manual
instrument—with 118 stops and nearly 7,000 pipes laid out in
seven storeys—received the accolade of that carrier of the Bach
tradition, Adolphe Hesse: 'the most perfect, most harmonious,
the largest and really the masterpiece of modern organ building'.[8]

Widor took up his new post on the eve of a particularly turbulent period in modern French history: the Franco–Prussian War
of 1870 and its aftermath. During the German siege of Paris from
September 1870 to January 1871, the services at Saint-Sulpice
went on with increased fervour; however, during a week of
bombardment in which the roof was pierced in two places, they
were held in the crypt.[9] Widor, who had not yet completed his
compulsory period of military service in the artillery, found
himself stationed at the garrison of Saint-Denis, to the North of
Paris.[10] This came under heavy fire during an attack, and the
casualties were heavy. Each Sunday, however, he was permitted
to return behind the lines to play at Saint-Sulpice in uniform.

The worst was to come. Having made an armistice with the
Germans, the newly elected National Assembly withdrew to
Versailles. Paris became the prey of the Communards, minority
extremist groups, who killed Archbishop Darboy and took over
many churches as political clubs. On 6 May 1871, a service to
celebrate the Month of the Virgin Mary was in progress at Saint-
Sulpice. Two Communards accompanied by Federal Guards tried
to force the large congregation to leave, but met with an
astonishing show of resistance. A club only succeeded in estab-
lishing itself with great difficulty. The next evening, there were
more disturbances as both worshippers and club members

struggled to enter the church, but on this occasion, the club was forced to withdraw.

On the following day, the battle raged inside Saint-Sulpice from the early hours. In the account of V. P. Fontoulieu,[11] 'The Club members showed off by roaring out the *Marseillaise*, and the faithful thundered out the *Magnificat*; The *Song of the Girondins* was answered by the *Salve Regina*.' Both sides resorted to physical violence. 'Then suddenly, a voice rose up over the others singing the *Parce Domine*; in this voice there was such power and charm that instinctively, all fell silent.' Eventually, the congregation gave way on the advice of the Curé, who had received warning that the Federal Guards had orders to fire in the event of further resistance. However, an arrangement was reached whereby the services could be held at earlier times in the day when the newly-styled *Club de la Victoire* was not in session.

The Club was finally brought to an end on 28 May with the entry into Paris by Government troops advancing along the nearby rue Vaugiraud. Widor himself described that harrowing time while the Commune was being put down with great loss of life and destruction of buildings: 'Everything was burning around us. Every day we expected to be roasted. But we beheld the spire of the Sainte-Chapelle constantly standing amid the flames. It was like a symbol of France remaining above these terrible events.'[12]

Saint-Sulpice survived without further damage. Amid the general feelings of relief, Widor gave vent to his youthful exuberance. In October 1871, Gabriel Fauré was appointed 'Petit Organiste', and he and Widor indulged themselves with friendly contests of improvisation on their respective instruments during services, of which the congregation remained unaware. Each found inspiration in the themes of the other. But it may well have been here that the seeds of the subsequent tensions between them were sown. In January 1874, Fauré left to become Saint-Saëns's assistant at the Madeleine, but the contests continued with his successor at Saint-Sulpice, André Messager.[13]

Over the decades, as Widor's musical and social reputation grew, a constant stream of distinguished visitors climbed the circular staircase to the organ loft. As Cavaillé-Coll's children have recorded, 'All the fashionable and artistic aristocracy were represented there; [the painter] Carolus Duran never failed to thunder out the *Domine salvum fac* at the top of his voice.'[14]

The Prince of Wales (later King Edward VII) came and presented Widor with an etching of Handel.[15] But not the least of these was that generous spirit, César Franck, who, as Marcel Dupré has told us, 'on Sunday mornings came back on foot from Sainte-Clotilde to his home on the Boulevard Saint-Michel, and often stopped off at Saint-Sulpice to wait for his friend at the bottom of the organ staircase'.[16]

The sight of Widor at his elegantly designed semicircular console—which he jocularly likened to the Roman Coliseum or a chemist's shop—was most impressive. He kept its metal parts well polished and covered it with a red carpet when not in use. While he prepared his registration, he would chat and joke with his friends, but when he played, his concentration was total. He sat, in the description of Louis Vierne,

immobile in the centre of the stool, his body lightly leaning forward. When he pulled stops, his movements were mathematically ordered so as to cause the minimum loss of time . . . his hands like sculpture, admirably cared for . . . no fruitless gesture ever disturbed the visual harmony, constantly in accord with the sonorous harmony.[17]

Once however, the effect was broken by Baron d'Erlanger's young son, who tumbled onto the pedal-board in the middle of the 'Offertoire': 'Dissonances were not yet in fashion, and this uncalled-for improvisation was not to the taste of the organist or my parents.'[18]

Other visitors have recorded their impressions. Paul Landormy, critic and violinist who played chamber music with Widor, described how he would

always remember those astonishing Christmas Eves, that midnight Mass overflowing with people, brilliantly illuminated and resounding with singing and the sumptuous sonorities of the organ . . . Widor played . . . a *Fantasie* of his own on a series of popular carols, which was a masterpiece of musical imagination and registration, a perpetual surprise, an enchantment.[19]

Frederic B. Stiven, Professor of Music in the University of Illinois, was resident in Paris in 1911. He recalled a Vespers on the Feast of the Assumption:

Widor began to improvise brilliantly in a march rhythm . . . altar boys in their red cassocks and white cottas bearing lighted candles . . . were followed by young men swinging burning censers in rhythm with the march . . . then the young girls . . . made a beautiful picture as they marched proudly down the long aisle, in their white dresses and flowing veils. [20]

During the sermons and after services animated conversations and arguments would take place in the exquisite little room which Widor had created behind the organ, hung with pictures of Cavaillé-Coll and former organists of the church, such as Nivers, Clérambault, and Sejan, as well as a bust of J. S. Bach. [21]

But at one time in the 1880s, Widor had been so overwhelmed by his admirers that his position was put at risk. The aesthete, Comte Robert de Montesquiou was dazzled by the sight of the Comtesse Potocka sitting on the organ stool turning his pages: 'was Seraphitus going to burn his wings for this demon?', mused the Comte. [22] According to the society painter, Jacques-Emile Blanche, Widor

played at High Mass on Sundays and Feast Days, [and] attracted music lovers as if it were a concert. Society ladies were behaving with so little decorum that the Archbishop of Paris forbade ladies to go up to the organ . . . the newspapers published reports which drew more fashionable audiences to Saint-Sulpice, and Monseigneur replaced Widor. He was forgotten. Then, forgiven, he recommenced his recitals. [23]

This account in reality records the spate of rumours flying around, for the registers of the *Conseil de Fabrique* 1870-88 make no mention of any dismissal, and Widor's salary of 2,000 francs was paid without interruption. But no doubt he received a rebuke and a warning from his Curé.

Certainly, a considerable number of movements of his earlier organ symphonies possess the popular qualities which attracted the ladies, whether they be the rousing 'Marches' and 'Finals', or the languishing salon-type pieces. Yet, for all his need as an ambitious young man to attract attention and be admired, he never lost sight of his higher musical vision. His scheme for an entire cycle of eight symphonies—based on a rising scale of tonalities from C to B, extending through the Op. 13 set and the later Op. 42 set (with Nos. 4 and 5 sharing the key of F)—is both a homage to Bach's *Well-Tempered Clavier* and an indication of the importance which he attached to organ composition.

The four symphonies of the Op. 42 set, first published in 1887, [24] show evidence of having been conceived as unified compositions rather than collections of individual pieces. They are also more genuinely symphonic than those from Op 13 in their sustained musical argument and their contrasts and conflicts of ideas. Their predominantly secular-humanist character would suggest that Widor conceived them in terms of his recitals rather than as an adjunct to the liturgy of the church.

Symphonie No. 5 in F minor is a most inspired and inventive work in which Widor gives free rein to his fecund gift of melody. The theme of the Allegro vivace is remarkable for its subtle tonal ambiguity worthy of C. P. E. Bach and Haydn: it opens in the 'wrong key' of the subdominant and only briefly touches the tonic before moving to the relative major. In the ensuing variations, Schumann's influence is apparent in the wealth of rhythmic invention and passages of propulsive dotted rhythms, snappy repeated chords, and humming semiquavers.

The ambience of the salon is reflected in the conventional beauty and elegance of the middle movements: the lyrical Allegro cantabile with its pianistic broken-chord textures; the Andantino quasi allegretto, its grave dignity compromised by ostinato passages in the pedals recalling the comical bassoon writing in the Finale of Beethoven's Symphony No. 8; and the more contrapuntal Adagio.

The final 'Toccata'—for which Widor's name is known to millions— is not of the Baroque type (as in No. 4); with its moto perpetuo flow of semiquavers, it is more akin to Schumann's *Toccata* for piano. As the steady pace of Widor's own recording (1932) reveals, this is not a mere showpiece. Its qualities are enhanced when it is played in the context of the whole symphony: the pedal entry of the theme with its two-octave 'drop' is then heard as a logical development of the octave-based motives in the first and third movements.

The Symphonie No. 6 in G minor is a work of greater weight and seriousness. The Allegro is based on creative oppositions and interactions between a monumental choral-type section and an expansive and turbulent Bach-inspired 'Fantasia' generating a ceaseless flow of triplet quavers. A striking and complex passage—thrown into relief by being in the key of F# minor, balancing a previous modulation to B♭ minor—is reached, in which these two elements are combined with fascinating cross-rhythms.

The Adagio in B major has, for modern tastes, an aura of sentimental piety with its registration for gambas and voix celestes and chromatically-inflected main theme. The atmosphere darkens with an enharmonic modulation to A♭ minor for the central section in which passages of Lisztian quasi-recitative and rugged two-part counterpoint emerge. In the gossamer 'Intermezzo', characterized by deft pianistic broken chords, Widor's sense of humour is allowed to bubble up. The fantasia element returns in the glorious Bachian 'Cantabile'—subtly distanced by its D♭ major tonality—as a florid obbligato to the melody.

The 'Finale' opens deceptively with a formal rondo theme consisting of ceremonial style tonic and dominant chords in the 'wrong key' of the subdominant. However, the nervous tension and demonic thrust of the episodes threatens to break out of this tidy classical scheme. Most remarkable is a passage with enormously widely-spaced part-writing, stark exposure of the fifth and tritone, and corruscating chromatic lines.[25]

Under the Abbé Hamon's successor, the Abbé Méritan (Curé, 1875-99), Saint-Sulpice was chosen to be the Centre for the Crusade against the treatment of blacks in Equitorial Africa, led by the Primate of Africa, the redoubtable Cardinal Lavigerie; and also for the *Institution de l'Archiconfrérie de Notre Dame de Compassion* for the conversion of England. The latter had been the dream of Olier 250 years earlier, whose efforts to convert the exiled King Charles II were in vain. A magnificent ceremony on 17 October 1897 was attended by a vast throng of over 10,000 people; the Archbishops of Paris and Westminster sat on thrones on either side of the altar. The climax consisted of 'a brilliant musical salute and the blessing of the Saint-Sacrement'.[26]

Widor had a Handelian sense of occasion. Even as a flamboyant young man, he understood perfectly the nature and requirements of the liturgy. Although his duties were confined to playing the 'Grand Orgue', he contributed a number of splendid choral works to the church's repertoire. He was fully alive to the opportunities for antiphonal effects in the Venetian style which the Seminarians together with the main choir made possible, in addition to the two organs at the opposite ends of the church. His festive *Messe* Op. 36 for double choir and two organs—which reflects so precisely the Sulpician emphasis on the praise of God—became the prototype for others by Vierne, Saint-Martin,

and Langlais. Some of Widor's motets also exploit these
resources, and all are refreshingly free of the sentimentality and
bombast prevalent at that time. Of these, noteworthy are 'Regina
Coeli', Op. 18 with its gloriously long-breathed vocal lines, the
Mozartian elegance of 'Tantum Ergo', Op. 18, and 'Tu es
Petrus', Op. 23 with massive blocks of harmony to symbolize the
rock on which Christ built his church.

With the passing of the years, plainchant struck an increasingly
profound response in Widor, and it formed the basis of his
celebrated improvisations described by Bernard Gavoty as 'great
liturgical frescos—two of his symphonies, the *Gothique* and the
Romane give as just an idea of them as possible'.[27] Widor realized
the indivisibility of the words and music in plainchant. It was his
intent when improvising versets in the Gloria, Gradual, and
Antiphons that 'the superb rhythm of the pedal, when the organ
responds to the choir, should emphasise the text and sustain it in
outbursts of exultation'.[28]

Louis Vierne—himself a master of the art—wrote of his
'memories of the *Sorties* after High Mass or Vespers at Saint-
Sulpice; I should say moreover, that to the last day of his titulariat
he manifested the same lucid gift; the last *Sortie* which I heard
him improvise in 193[3] left me spellbound; he had something
special, I assure you'.[29] But it must not be forgotten that the
works of J. S. Bach remained his staple diet and ultimate criterion
of musical value.

Widor came to regard Saint-Sulpice as his home. Before leaving
the church, he would, as Isador Philipp tells us,

pause with his friends before the magnificent murals painted by Delacroix
. . . making his friends admire them. 'Isn't it beautiful, isn't it splendid',
he would cry, 'isn't this worthy of Rubens?' And he would go to the
[chamber organ] of Marie Antoinette which he had placed in one of the
small chapels, and would play a few measures of the Mozart Sonata in A,
saying over and over: 'Yes, yes, he was the god of music.'[30]

Amid the counterpoint, as it were, of his extraordinarily varied
life, Saint-Sulpice stood like a veritable cantus firmus.

4

SOCIETY AND POLITICS

FOR all his cosmopolitan, nomadic ancestry, Widor loved Paris.
During his first visits there in the 1860s the capital was under-
going its radical reconstruction at the hands of Baron
Haussmann. But Widor did not make his home in one of the
newly built apartments: the well-preserved Latin Quarter, with its
wealth of artistic and historical associations, was much more to
his taste.

With limited financial means at his disposal, Widor's dreams of
aristocratic grandeur had to be tempered with reality. His first
home consisted of rooms in the magnificent Hotel de Sourdéac,
built in 1646 at 8 rue Garancière, where the Marquis de
Sourdéac—one of the first Directors of the Opéra—had made a
small theatre. From 1818-49, it was the Mairie of the old XI
Arrondissement. But by the time Widor moved in, it was largely
office accommodation which lay behind that noble façade.[1] On
the ground floor, he had his 'den', a large room containing a
grand piano with an Erard pedal attachment, a table, and three
chairs. On the walls hung a sketch of Widor by his friend Carolus
Duran, paintings and drawings by Van Dyke, Guercino,
Rembrandt, and Delacroix, and signed photographs of his cousin
Paul Bourget and Guy de Maupassant. A charming watercolour
by James Tissot bore a dedication 'for the memory of the Sunday
lunches and the music before Vespers, June 1891'.[2]

After his appointment as Professor at the Paris Conservatoire,
Widor moved in 1893 into more spacious, if less Romantic
quarters at 3 rue de l'Abbaye (now part of the Institut Catholique).
Its rather forbidding institutional exterior, however, hides a
pleasant rear courtyard lined with trees, overlooking Saint-
Germain-des-Prés. In his suite on the ground floor he installed a
superb chamber organ built by Cavaillé-Coll; and 'a secret door,
for a mysterious purpose, opened into a little alley'.[3]

For most of his long life, Widor remained a bachelor, for he considered that 'the true artist is hardly made for marriage'.[4] Treasuring his freedom from economic dependents and the overriding need to earn money, which so constricted the lives of many musicians like Franck, he only took the plunge into matrimony at an advanced age. Not that he had no liking for the fair sex: on the contrary, he was a highly-sexed man who indulged in a number of affairs. His pupil, Edgard Varèse, liked to recall the morning when he arrived at his house for a private lesson. Widor, half-dressed, excused himself: 'Pardon, Varèse, I can't receive you, I have company.'[5]

Widor did not conform to the popular image of a church organist, in contrast with Franck and his formal shabby clothes. The younger man was urbane and sophisticated: spurning respectable bourgeois black, he sported a blue suit with a spotted cravat and a soft hat.[6] As an ambitious man making his way in the musical world, with some success in the glittering fields of opera and ballet, he could also serve the church on the aesthetic and ceremonial levels. But he was not prepared to be placed into intellectual or social straightjackets. Indeed, he strayed into areas of ideas and politics where a good Catholic would have feared to tread. He even claimed to believe in the transmigration of souls, having had an intuition during a country walk that, in a former existence, he had been a duck swimming on a pond![7] Spiritualism was at that time a fashionable cult among scientists and politicians opposed to the church, like Ferry and Combes, not to mention the venerable poet, Victor Hugo, whom Widor admired.[8]

Nevertheless, he had a sceptical cast of mind, essentially practical and with a strong sense of reality. Among his closest friends were painters and writers of the Naturalist school, observing man and nature with a scientific detachment: Maupassant, master of the short story, Bourget, penetrating critic and novelist, François Coppée, the '*poète des humbles*' who developed his own deliberately plain style, and Carolus Duran, 'the French Velasquez', celebrated for his portraits of fashionable women but at the expense of his Realist inclinations, for which he was attacked by Zola. In his own outward coldness of manner, frequently commented on, Widor reflected their 'Parnassian' reserve, in marked reaction to the Romantic flamboyance of the previous generation of Hugo, Delacroix, Berlioz, and Liszt.

Widor's own interest in literature, art, and politics was immense, and he revelled in conversation and discussion. But he was too optimistic and ambitious by nature to share the morbid anxieties of Bourget, obsessed as he was with his generation's 'moral crisis' and absence of hope.[9] Maupassant, too, was consumed by pessimism and despair. In contrast, Widor (in the words of Imbert) 'believes in his star. But the glory of which he dreams is not that of those who can talk to him about disturbing subjects.'[10]

Widor was fascinated by the *beau monde* and its display of wealth and power. Like Marcel Proust, he was an observer of life and an assiduous attender of salons. The world of high politics provided endless interest. A burning question was whether the Catholic Church in France would continue the post-Revolution reaction of Joseph de Maistre which stressed absolute authority, discipline, and repression of the critical intelligence. Unlike the Oxford Movement in England, the French Catholic revival was highly politicized, supporting the Restoration of the Monarchy and the doctrine of Ultramontanism. Nevertheless, there were a significant number of Liberal Catholics—like Widor's friend, the politician Etienne Lamy—who worked for the adaptation of the church to modern democratic society.[11]

The salons had their own exclusive allegiances and antipathies, and Widor succeeded in treading the narrow tightropes between them to a considerable extent. Those of the old aristocratic families supported the Catholic Church and its political pretensions, whereas the upper bourgeois—the bankers, doctors, and architects—formed the pillars of the Third Republic with its belief in liberalism and free scientific enquiry.[12]

Widor's entry into society was gained through his musical ability and also his powers of conversation, despite a lisp. With his keen wit, he could readily hold his own. To the rather disagreeable Viscomtesse de Trédern, he once retorted: 'Madame, may I dare to ask you to mingle in your conversation a little of that sugar which your father manufactures so well?'[13] On another occasion, Widor was himself the victim of an excellent practical joke played by his Yorkshire pupil, J. W. Ibberson. A distinguished visitor to Paris, also a Yorkshireman, was to meet Widor at a reception. The latter, wishing to greet him in English, applied to Ibberson. The visitor was duly welcomed with the words 'Nah then Lad, 'ow artta?', to his amusement and Widor's embarrassment. [14]

Widor was frequently to be found at the salon of Madame Bertin, the widow of Edouard Bertin, proprietor of the respectable conservative newspaper *Journal des Débats*. This had stirring associations as Berlioz had been on its staff as a writer of concert and theatre notices, and had benefited from the support of Edouard's father, Louis. [15] After the establishment of the Third Republic, the paper opposed Ultramontanism and Clericalism from its position on the centre left. [16]

At this salon, Widor claimed to have met most of the great men at the end of the Romantic era:

> For more than fifty years, Mme. Bertin had received in her town-house, today divided into 7 and 7b rue de Saint-Pères, all who were regarded as distinguished representatives of letters, politics, the sciences and the arts: Hugo, Ingres, Berlioz, Delacroix, then Gounod, Saint-Saëns, Bizet, Daubigny, Corot, Bonnat . . . her high culture, intelligence and memory won the admiration of us all. [17]

Very stimulating intellectually was the Salon Orfila presided over by Marie Trélat, married into a leading family of doctors and architects. [18] It was justly known as the 'Headquarters of Positivism', being a meeting-place for distinguished scientists, freethinkers, and liberal politicians, including Ernest Renan, author of the controversial *La Vie de Jésus*, which presented Christ in a purely Humanist light, and the Opportunist politician Jules Ferry, a highly cultivated lover of music who had known Liszt and Wagner. Widor and Ferry became firm friends.

Alternating between the posts of Minister of Public Instruction and Prime Minister between 1879 and 1885, Ferry implemented his policy of Sociability, the fostering of national unity and harmony by freeing state education from the hold of the Catholic Church. But he was not an atheist or hostile to religion *per se*— among his supporters were a number of Protestants, including Baron d'Erlanger. Ferry considered that 'all the stimulants which can strengthen moral teaching, whether they come from idealistic, spiritualist or even theological beliefs, all these supports are good'. [19] In 1889, he took over the daily newspaper *l'Estafette* to which Widor contributed music criticism under the *nom de plume* 'Aulètes'. But Ferry's attempt to use this paper of mediocre

importance to justify his unpopular policies proved a failure: its
journalists, under the editor Abel Peyrouton—an old revolutionary—were barely competent. [20]

Marie Trélat was a singer, to whom Fauré dedicated his well-
known 'Lydia', and Widor his Op. 14 set of songs. These include
the fine 'A cette terre' to Hugo's words. The turbulent setting of
the opening stanzas in G minor gives way to a final section in
G major, a lyrical effusion of simple romance with echoes of
Schumann's *Frauenliebe und Leben*. Widor felt a great affection
for her, expressed—within the proprieties of the times—in
the correspondence between them. ('I am thinking of you
ceaselessly.'[21]) *Le Ménéstrel* records a fascinating soirée at
her salon in February 1882: among the guests were the painters
Léon Bonnat and Carolus Duran, as well as Renan and Ferry.
The musical programme included two of Widor's 'Mélodies
italiennes', (from Opp. 32 and 35) sung by Marie Trélat and
Madame Ella Lemmens-Sherrington, wife of his old Professor in
Brussels, and celebrated for her oratorio performances. The
seductive Rosita Mauri, principal dancer at the Opera, danced the
'Sabiotière' from Widor's recently successful ballet score *La
Korrigane*. Both composer and dancer were acclaimed; Widor
himself accompanied the entire evening at the piano 'si bien,
si bien'. [22]

According to Proust, it seems that the doors of the old French
aristocracy—with its genealogical snobbery—were closed to
Widor. In his great social novel *A la recherche du temps perdu*,
Proust himself is mistaken for Widor by Monsieur de Bréauté
during a reception given for King Edward VII and Queen
Alexandra: 'For an instant, the name of M. Widor crossed his
mind; but he considered that I was much too young to be an
organist, and M. Widor not sufficiently notable to be received.' [23]
Yet, as we have seen in chapter 3, he did meet King Edward at
Saint-Sulpice, probably having been introduced by the King's
friends, M. and Mme Standish,[24] whose niece he was—many
years later—to marry.

The position was different in the case of foreign aristocrats who
had made their new home in Paris. The Princesse Rachel de
Brancovan, the daughter of the Turkish Ambassador to London,
Musurus Pacha, had married the Roumanian Prince Grégoire de
Brancovan. Her house in the Avenue Hoche reflected her exotic

origins. In the description by her daughter Anna de Noailles,

The main salon was lined with plush of a turquoise colour, and furnished with golden sofas and chairs. Two large rosewood pianos side by side displayed their polished gleams beneath a tall, wilting palm tree. On the other side of the vestibule, an oriental boudoir, shining and ringing, I should say, like jewels in a bazaar.[25]

This atmosphere of Eastern luxury drew a regular circle which included the poets Sully Prudhomme, Leconte de Lisle, Heredia, and Mistral. Later, Rachel became the model for Proust's character Madame de Cambremer, and the Polish pianist Paderewski was caught up in a passionate love affair with her.[26]

Rachel was an excellent pianist who had been a pupil of Camille O'Meara Dubois, one of Chopin's students. In June 1882, she accompanied Remi in a performance of Widor's Violin Sonata in C minor, Op. 50 which had been dedicated to her.[27] It is a power-ful, terse work with its opening theme in stark octave writing. But, in return for her attentions, her possessive nature claimed the undivided loyalty of her friends. Etienne Lamy felt compelled to decline a lunch party invitation from Widor in a revealing letter: 'I would have been delighted to be sitting between your *deux étoiles*, not to mention the poet and the musician. But I have promised that morning to our dear Princesse Brancovan; you know the price of this friendship and the grief I would suffer in disappointing her. . . .'[28]

The Comtesse Potocka, a fervent Royalist, held a fatal attrac-tion for Widor. Born Emmanuela Pignatelli, of a famous Roman family descended from Pope Innocent XII, she was the niece of Delphine Potocka, a pupil and friend of Chopin. Emmanuela and her husband, a Polish banker, soon grew apart from each other. Her salon in the Avenue Friedland became the venue for her riotous club, 'The Maccabees', which numbered Bourget, Maupassant, and the society painter Jacques-Emile Blanche among its members.[29] The last-named considered that the atmos-phere acted on Maupassant's brain, causing his final insanity. Justly known as 'The Siren', Emmanuela was a predatory female who used her famed beauty to trap unwary men. Blanche described her physical charms: 'Her broad, low forehead, her eyebrows, nose and mouth have the proportions of the Golden Section . . . Emmanuela's gaze was everything, in a face polished like an apple'.[30]

She was also an outstanding pianist who had studied with Liszt, and received the dedications of Fauré's *Impromptu* Op. 25, and Widor's Piano Quartet in A minor, Op. 66. The turbulent opening and the Lisztian piano writing of the latter was surely a reflection of her personality. Perhaps it was to escape from the Maccabees, or even to avoid further scandal after the episode at Saint-Sulpice, that Widor took her 'to make music' in an 'astonishing old building' in the rue de Valois. The celebrated aesthete Comte Robert de Montesquiou himself considered moving in there at her suggestion: 'its description gave me that little fever which accompanies great desires'. In the ground floor rooms, 'Olympuses tumble down on your head in cascades of nudes and draperies from the centre of domed ceilings, enhanced with old gold, and supported by pillars.'[31] After she moved to Auteil to care for her collection of stray dogs, Widor was one of a faithful band of followers who continued to visit her.[32]

For the Comtesse de Mailly Nestles, Widor composed his song-cycle *Soirs d'été* (1889) to poems by Bourget, selected from *Les Aveux* (1882). Here, Widor attempted to tackle the new climate of aesthetic sensibility of the 'decadent' poets—Verlaine and Mallarmé—with whom Bourget was associated. The poet offered advice to Widor on grouping the poems, and on a title: 'At no price *Poèmes Mélancoliques*. Call it *La Chanson du Regret*—an excellent title.'[33] In the end, neither of these were used. Widor's musical style, however, formed under the influence of the Austro-German tradition, was more suitable for the rhetoric of Hugo than the pale, almost Pre-Raphaelite quality of Bourget's verse:

> L'âme évaporée et souffrante,
> L'âme douce, l'âme odorante
> Des lys divins que j'ai cueillis
> Dans le jardin de ta pensée

There is a much more successful integration of words and music in Debussy's better-known setting of the same poem under the title 'Romance'. It was now that Fauré came into his own, outstripping his rival in the fields of song and chamber music. In his *Cinq Mélodies de Venise* (1889) and *La Bonne Chanson* (1892)—the former dedicated to the Princesse de Scey-Montbéliard (later the Princesse de Polignac) whose salon was rapidly becoming the magnet for the most advanced writers and composers[34]—Fauré fully succeeded in entering the shadows and half-lights of Verlaine. In 1893, Fauré himself cast aside his diffidence in a letter to the Vicomtesse Greffulhe: 'The opinion of Saint-Saëns is that I am the only one compared with Widor, Dubois, Joncières, Salvayre and Godard who has contributed, added something new to music.'[35]

However fascinating these hothouse worlds proved to be, Widor needed his own social base where he could relax with his bachelor friends. Foyot's restaurant (now closed) at 33 rue Tournon served this purpose admirably. Julian Street described it as

quiet, dignified, restrained; the lighting is low and agreeable, the carpets seem softer than in other places, one does not hear the waiters move about, and there is never a clatter of silverware and dishes. It is not an ostentatious place, and puts on no airs, yet to me it is the very embodiment of refinement and distinction. . . . Naturally, the cuisine and service are perfection, and the cellars are of the best. . . .[36]

Situated opposite the Senate in the Palais de Luxembourg, it was well patronized by politicians. In fact, as Philipp observed,

All intellectual Paris used to assemble there, and one might often see gathered about Widor's table the witty Alexandre Dumas, Calvé and Henri Cain, both highly amusing, the de Reszkés, the spiteful and malicious Forain, the sad and gloomy Maupassant, Albert Schweitzer and Busoni and Godowsky, when they were in Paris. Those were rare hours indeed.[37]

Widor was noted for his enormous appetite. When Tchaikovsky visited Paris in March 1888, he told his brother Modest that 'Widor gave me a huge meal.'[38] However, the organist's vast expenditure of energy ensured that he did not become obese. As he himself said jokingly to his pupil Louis Vierne on the latter's return from an organ recital tour of Holland: 'If your career continues in this accelerating rhythm, there is little chance that you will ever become fat: it's a therapy which one should recommend to pretty women concerned with the aesthetics of their figures.'[39]

5

WIDER AMBITIONS

WIDOR'S musical ambitions were by no means restricted to the church and the salon. The opera house and the concert platform presented an irresistible challenge to a superbly equipped musical all-rounder, notwithstanding the attendant dangers of the savagery of the critics, capricious public opinion, and the claque. But in the musical world of Paris, rent with cliques and factions, he 'took no sides, asking only to work in peace', as Philipp tells us.[1] For all his fascination with High Politics, the sordid intrigues of his profession held little appeal for one who totally lacked the necessary low cunning.

Although Widor had a great capacity for friendship, it seems that his isolated existence as a student in Brussels had reinforced his natural self-sufficiency, and given him a horror of being submerged within a group. Thus he was not among the founders of the *Société Nationale* brought into being in 1871 to promote the work of French composers. On the other hand, he was on excellent terms with most of them as individuals—Lalo, Massenet, Bizet, Franck, Saint-Saëns, and (to begin with) Fauré. The last-named increasingly became Widor's chief rival and thus tended to come between him and Saint-Saëns, who guarded the fortunes of his old pupil like a dragon.

In the case of Franck, the situation was particularly complicated. Here, Widor had a delicate tightrope to tread, for another of his friends and allies was Ambroise Thomas, the Director of the Paris Conservatoire, who came to regard Franck, his Professor of Organ, with open contempt.[2] Moreover, Franck's embarrassingly pugnacious disciples—headed by Vincent d'Indy—turned away violently from the original *Société Nationale* group. Unlike his fellow organists Guilmant, Gigout, and Dubois (who were to receive the dedications of Franck's *Trois Chorals*), Widor did not become embroiled in this Franckist movement to any extent. Indeed, its self-righteous dogmatism can only have been distasteful to his sceptical mind. His aloofness from faction, too, was consistent with his eclectic philosophy of appreciating the best in everything.

That blazing comet in the musical firmament, Richard Wagner, drew an adventurous French contingent to Bayreuth in 1876 for the first complete performance of *Der Ring des Nibelungen*. Widor was there, in the company of Baron d'Erlanger—still a devoted Wagnerite despite debts still accruing from the Paris *Tannhäuser* fiasco, and the resulting bad feeling.[3] At the end of his life, Widor humorously recalled the effect of the music on him: he spent the performances admiring the bare shoulders of Madame Wolkenstein, the wife of the Prussian Ambassador to St Petersburg, who was sitting in front of him beside Liszt. Years later he told her![4]

Widor's first meeting with Liszt took place on that occasion, although, to his regret, he was not destined to make the acquaintance of Wagner himself. In Marcel Dupré's account,

At the first interval in the *Twilight of the Gods*, the great pianist was anxious to know whether he had ever been introduced to Wagner. The answer being no, 'well, meet me here in the next interval and we will go together.' On reaching the stage, they saw at the rear, Wagner who was small, standing before the singer playing the role of Hagen [Gustav Siehr], a gigantic demi-god made still taller by his helmet . . . listening to the vehement reproaches of the master, accompanied by angry gestures. 'You see, this isn't the right moment', murmured Liszt, as they made themselves scarce.[5]

Widor did not, however, miss further opportunities to experience Wagner's music dramas. During a visit to Vienna in 1882—during which he dined with the brother of the Empress—he heard *Lohengrin* and *Meistersinger* at the Opera. The latter, in its diatonic splendour, was his favourite: 'in spite of some longueurs, it is admirable, Wagner's masterpiece undoubtedly. A magnificent performance by the singers, the orchestra unbelievedly perfect, one could not obtain its equal in Paris. The timpani roll like thunder, the horns sound like trombones, exploding in fanfares to shame the hunting horns of our *Mardi Gras*!'[6]

Soon after Bayreuth, Widor renewed his contact with Liszt at the 1878 International Exhibition in Paris, which marked the economic revival of France after the defeat of 1870. A fantastic

Moorish style palace, the Trocadéro, was specially built with a magnificent Cavaillé-Coll organ which was inaugurated with Franck's *Trois Pièces*, commissioned for the occasion. The instrument was proved and tested by members of the international jury, among them Liszt representing Hungary and Helmholtz representing Germany. The Rosette and the Great Medal of Honour was awarded to Cavaillé-Coll as the outstanding organ-builder represented at the Exhibition, which also included work by Merklin, Abbey, Stoltz, and Fermis.[7]

When Liszt was due to try the organ, Cavaillé-Coll sent for Widor to assist him. According to Dupré,

Liszt began to play the organ, admiring its beautiful sonorities. Then he asked [Widor] to play some of [his] own compositions for him to listen to in the hall . . . Liszt said to [him], 'You have been very kind to devote this morning to me . . . What can I do to thank you?' 'Maître, if I could listen to you play the piano for only five minutes'.

With characteristic generosity, Liszt invited him to be present during his practice times at his suite at 13 rue du Mail, which Madame Erard—widow of the celebrated piano manufacturer— had put at his disposal.

For six consecutive days, I heard Liszt play the entire piano repertoire from the early works right through to the modern ones of that time, like Balakirev's *Islamey*. He knew them all by heart. His playing had an unspeakable grandeur. He played with low wrists, and his huge hands were spread out on the keyboard like fans.[8]

Liszt, great encourager of other composers as he was, continued to take an interest in his young acquaintance, not least because of Widor's Hungarian origins. Widor's Trio Op. 19 was performed at Weimar with Liszt himself taking the piano part. The latter privately expressed his opinion of the work to Olga von Meyendorff: 'Widor's *Trio*, while distinguished, does not seem to me to be on the same level as those by Saint-Saëns and Bronsart.'[9]

Meanwhile, Widor continued to inaugurate Cavaillé-Coll's organs, of which over 600 were installed throughout France and Europe during the builder's lifetime. In 1879, he gave the opening recital on the new organ at the Brussels Conservatoire.[10] Yet, for all his faithful following at Saint-Sulpice, as an organist he seems to have been overshadowed by Guilmant, who held a very successful regular series of Organ Concerts with orchestra at the Trocadéro, in collaboration with the conductor Edouard Colonne. Guilmant, who also did sterling work as an archivist, presented enterprising *Summaries of the History of the Organ from 1586 to the Present Day*, which included long-lost works by such composers as A. Gabrielli, Merulo, Titelouze, Frescobaldi, and Clérembault.[11] The culmination of these efforts lay in the publication of his *Ecole Classique de l'Orgue* (1898-1903) and the *Archives des Maîtres de l'Orgue des 16e, 17e 18e siècles* (1898-1914) with introductions by Widor's pupil and friend, the musicologist André Pirro.

In December 1880, however, Widor established himself before the public in a completely different sphere. His score for the ballet *La Korrigane*, mounted at the Opéra, was described by Philipp as 'a little masterpiece, as refined and alluring as the *Coppélia* of Delibes'.[12] The story, devised by Coppée, is a version of Cinderella set in seventeenth-century Brittany. The leading role of the servant-girl Yvonnette was a triumph for Rosita Mauri, who stole the heart of Baron d'Erlanger's adolescent son.[13] The honours were in fact evenly distributed between her and the composer, and the music of *La Korrigane* continued to be played in various arrangements throughout his lifetime.

A few years later, Franck asked Widor for his opinion on some ballet music (probably for the ill-starred opera *Hulda*) which he had just written: 'I think one can dance to it very well, for last night I had my wife play it for me on the piano, and I danced to it before the mirror in my nightshirt!' Widor was amused but not impressed.[14] Also unfruitful was Franck's serious proposition to Widor in 1880. The older man coveted a Professorship of Composition at the Conservatoire and asked him to use his influence with Ferry, the Minister of Public Instruction, to obtain this post for him; then Widor could step into his shoes in the organ class. But he did not jump at the chance: 'I was very young, very ignorant of the methods of teaching at the Conservatoire, afraid to assume the heavy responsibility', as he admitted much later.[15]

The 1880s produced a number of stage works from the organist of Saint-Sulpice. In September 1885, Auguste-Léon Dorchain's play *Conte d'avril* (after Shakespeare's Twelfth Night) was put on at the Odéon with Widor's incidental music. In Philipp's view,

'This score placed Widor in the top rank. It was a long time since a new work so pure and charming had been heard.'[16]

Two months later, Coppée's historical verse-drama *Les Jacobites* opened at the Odéon, again with incidental music by Widor. Coppée's biographer, de Lescure, has described how

none of his colleagues and friends invited one evening in October 1885, will forget the impressions of that party where the guests at a hearty dinner became the poet's rapt audience. It was impossible for them to listen without emotion, enthusiasm or applause to him reading the five Acts of *Les Jacobites* in succession—with five breaks for cigarettes—in his warm and vibrant voice . . . myself, Jules Clarette, Paul Bourget, Louis Depret, Louis Gandérax and Widor unanimously predicted its desired success.

Unfortunately, the effect of the play in performance was weakened by the variable quality of the acting.[17]

The sombre mood of *Les Jacobites* anticipates Widor's first full-scale opera *Maître Ambros*, a work of serious musical and dramatic aspirations, in marked contrast with the lightweight charm and easy tunefulness of *La Korrigane* and *Conte d'avril*. Its production, by Léon Carvalho, took place at the Opéra-Comique in May 1886. The libretto, by Coppée and Dorchain, is set in the mid-seventeenth century Dutch Republic. The authoritarian Calvinist William II of Orange has mounted a *coup d'état* against the powerful Burghers. The Civil Guard, enlisting the aid of the intrepid seafarer Maître Ambros, sing the opening chorus 'We will resist William of Orange, he is our Stadholder, not our King!' Plans to attack Nassau, however, are undermined by the rivalry between Ambros and Hendrick the Burghmaster for the love of Nella.

The most striking aspect of the opera lies perhaps in the Meyerbeerian opportunities for crowd scenes and visual effects presented by the patriotic choruses: of these, particularly impressive is the 'Blessing of the Flags' in Act III, in which the bellicose songs of the soldiers contrast effectively with the chorus of women in the church, singing a quasi-plainchant melody.

The reactions of the critics were generally favourable, if a little guarded. It is amusing today to read how they automatically attributed any bold or unusual feature of melody or harmony to the 'Wagnerian Revolution'. With some degree of exaggeration, the *Télégraphe* considered the opera to be 'a score of complex

encies half-way between German innovations and the
lic tradition, a sort of semi-Wagnerian adaptation'.[18]

rsions into the public arena gave Widor some
... of the worldly success which he craved, and at the same
time, the confidence to pursue his uncompromising vision of
organ composition. His organ symphonies Nos. 7 and 8 (of the
Op. 42 set) are characterized by a high level of cogent musical
argument, surely reflecting the experience of handling the
orchestra and the dramatic requirements of stage works. In both
symphonies, moreover, there is a considerable degree of motivic
unity between movements, anticipating the use of cyclic themes
in the final symphonies, 'Gothique' and 'Romane'.

Symphonie No. 7 in A minor is a tough and uncompromising
work of startling originality for its time. The Moderato, a terse
but unorthodox sonata-form movement, has for its first subject a
violent passage of jagged syncopated semiquavers in stark
octaves. In the second subject, in the unusual key of the subdominant, these agitated rhythms reappear in a dramatic rising
line while a new lyrical theme quietly unfolds in the background.
In the development and recapitulation, this theme emerges into
greater prominence as the rhythmic turbulence subsides.

The 'Choral' became the model for the similar movement in
the Symphonie No. 2 of Louis Vierne. Conflict is set up between
a sublime hymn in A major—based on a descending figure E D C
B A, variants of which shape many of the themes in the remaining movements—and an agitated section in A minor. The
Andante allegretto (in F # minor) is a pastoral in trio-sonata style:
its contrasting sections evoke the musette with long pedal points.
The Allegro ma non troppo (in A minor) has the appearance of a
rigid Baroque structure, yet a Romantic intimacy of feeling is con-
veyed by the expressive melody and flow of murmuring semiquavers outlining sensuous harmonies. The contrasting rich
texture of five-part counterpoint gives the Lento (in C # minor) its
Bachian gravity. The 'Finale' (in A minor) is a unique conception. The powerful main theme is stated in the pedals below
strident bell-like open fifths. Later, Widor brings off a *tour de
force* with a corruscating carillon effect, achieved by a prolonged
ostinato, gradually wound down with enormous tension.

Symphonie No. 8 in B major is, in terms of the organ repertoire,
arguably comparable in stature to Beethoven's 'Hammerklavier'

Sonata, Op. 106 and Liszt's Sonata in B minor in its monumental scale and transcendental exploitation of the instrument. The Allegro is a massive sonata-form structure. The first subject's brilliant bursts of diatonic harmony—with powerful pedal-points and extended trills—overshadows the brief pleading second subject theme with its rising chromatic bass. A titanic central development leads into the irregular recapitulation, in which the second subject is engulfed by a further section of dramatic development.

The Moderato cantabile (in E major) resembles the 'In Paradisium' of Fauré's *Requiem* (1886) with its suave melody accompanied by broken chords on the voix celeste. The lively scherzo-like Allegro is full of canonic invention. Contrapuntal mastery is also evident in the massive 'Variations' movement (in D minor) based on a robust theme stated in the pedals. Monotony is skilfully avoided by textural variety, including rapid scalic passages and pianistic chordal writing, which—despite their complexity—always preserve clarity. The expressive theme of the Adagio (in F # major) unfolds above a double pedal-point in fifths in an atmosphere of uneasy calm; the restless central section opens with a terse fugato. The Finale has a hard-edged sheen and fiery spirit. In the closing bars, a shatteringly dissonant appoggiatura sums up the rigours of this symphonie, one of Widor's greatest.

During the 1880s Widor undertook what may be best described as a labour of love. Unlike England and Germany, France had never boasted a fine indigenous choral tradition, with the result that little opportunity presented itself for performance of its great repertoire there. In 1873, the conductor Charles Lamoureux—inspired by the massive choral forces assembled in London's Crystal Palace—set up his own Société Harmonie Sacrée in Paris, performing Handel's *Messiah* and Bach's *St Matthew Passion* at the Cirque d'Eté. In spite of considerable public interest, this enterprise foundered for lack of financial resources at the end of the decade.[19]

At this point, Widor took up the challenge. With Gounod and Henriette Fuchs, the wife of an engineer, he founded the Société Concordia, with singers largely drawn from the Alsatian community in Paris.[20] Its aim was 'to lend its assistance to modern composers, and above all bring to light masterpieces the performances of which require the co-operation of forces which the individual initiative can only bring together with difficulty'. [21] Widor himself was its conductor, directing rehearsals with the greatest care and attention to detail: the choral sound 'showed evidence in turn of warmth, enthusiasm and delicacy', in the judgment of *Le Ménéstrel*. [22] The original rehearsal pianist, Paul Vidal, was in 1883 succeeded by the more difficult and temperamental Claude Debussy until his departure for Rome in January 1885. [23]

A most interesting variety of works was performed under Widor's baton, including Haydn's *The Seasons* (1882), Liszt's *St Elizabeth* (1882), Mendelssohn's *Athalia* (1883), Schumann's *Paradise and the Peri* (1885), and Saint-Saëns's *Christmas Oratorio* (1889). The regular soprano soloist was Madame Fuchs, an experienced amateur singer who had given the premières of Fauré's 'Après un rêve', 'Sylvie', 'Nell', and 'Automne' at the Société Nationale [24]: she was universally known as 'The Soul of the Concordia'.

The most ambitious work to be tackled was surely Bach's *St Matthew Passion*, which received its second performance in France on 16 May 1888 at the Conservatoire. Widor took special pains over its preparation, even applying to Josef Joachim for advice. The great violinist and friend of Brahms regretted that he was too occupied with his teaching duties to respond to this request concerning 'St Jean Sebastien'. However, he ended on a positive note: 'The manner in which you will make it understood to your performers will speak for itself, and more so than my poor pen could contribute, with its scant familiarity with your difficult and subtle language.' [25] In the opinion of *Le Ménéstrel*, 'a few more rehearsals would not have been amiss for the orchestra. Nevertheless, Widor directed, if not with a sufficiently communicative warmth, at least with perfect precision and a profound knowledge of Bach's music.' [26]

The fate of the Concordia was similar to that of the Harmonie Sacrée: it was disbanded at the end of the decade through lack of vitality among its backers, according to Albert Schweitzer. Its library was offered for sale at a ridiculously low cost without finding a buyer. [27] Widor must have been bitterly disappointed: the sheer effort and organization expended had no permanent result.

It was to London that Widor looked for performances of his own orchestral music. In March 1887, August Mann included his Symphonie No. 2 in A, Op. 54—along with Bruch's Violin Concerto played by Joachim—in his series of concerts at the Crystal Palace. Widor's symphonie, scored for standard Romantic orchestral forces with full brass, is concise and incisive, but failed utterly to please the critics. The *Musical Times* wrote: 'We confess to being bitterly disappointed with Widor's symphony of which such favourable expectations had been aroused.'[28] As far as the 'Perfect Wagnerite', George Bernard Shaw, was concerned, 'Berlioz himself, in his most uninspired moments, could not have been more elaborately and intelligently dull.'[29]

Conducting was a bug that bit Widor badly, and we find him seeking every opportunity to direct performances of his own works. But, according to Philipp, he was 'a mediocre, uncertain, timid orchestral conductor, yet he liked to conduct, as if he, of all people, was in search of applause'.[30] In November 1887, he entered into correspondence with Francesco Berger, Secretary of the Royal Philharmonic Society of London. It was arranged between them that the Society would be given the world première of his symphonie 'La Nuit de Walpurgis' on 19 April 1888—one month before the *St Matthew Passion* in Paris! So eager was Widor to direct the performance himself that he expressed himself as being quite unconcerned with financial negotiations: 'I have no experience of your practices: I leave the Society free to do what it feels it should, the artistic question being of sole importance.'[31] In December, he wrote again: 'the expenses of the journey are most adequate, and I thank you, regretting that I am not rich enough to refuse them'.[32]

Further letters reveal Widor's efforts to ensure that his work suffered as little as possible from the inadequate rehearsal schedules. Nine days before the concert, the parts were sent off in advance 'in case the professors wish to look at their parts in view of the little time we shall have'.[33] True to form, he managed to combine business with pleasure, for during his visit to London he was the guest of Baron d'Erlanger's son at his home at 6 Hamilton Place, Piccadilly, and on the day before the concert, dined with the chief conductor of the Philharmonic Society, Frederic Cowen.[34]

In contrast with the classical formalism of the two earlier orchestral symphonies, 'La Nuit de Walpurgis' constituted a passing gesture towards Liszt's 'Music of the Future' with its programme based on an episode from the *locus classicus* of German Romanticism, Goethe's *Faust*. Composed in three movements, the extraordinary inventiveness of the orchestral textures owes much to Berlioz's *Symphonie Fantastique*. The 'Overture' depicts Faust and Mephistopheles ascending a mountain amid the fury of the elements evoked by a panoply of complex rhythmic groupings, rapid chromatic scales, tremolos, and extremes of dynamics. The mood of the serene Adagio, in which Helen appears before Paris, is set by a mysterious diminished seventh chord on high muted strings and harp. In the final 'Bacchanale', the unholy revels inspired a fantastic dance movement.

Not content with half-measures, Widor also provided a pretentious programme-note so uncharacteristic of his usual down-to-earth mentality that we can only assume it to have been a publicity gesture—or perhaps even a debunking of woolly metaphysics—rather than a serious statement of artistic intent! In the account of the *Musical Times*, 'Mr Widor makes a great parade of the meaning to be attached to his themes, bidding us recognise one as expressing the general philosophic idea of the work, accept another as the "phrase morale", a third as the "note sentimentale", and so on.'[35] Although the music purported to be specially composed for this occasion, in fact another (unpublished) work of the same name—consisting of an 'Overture', 'Andante', and 'Danse de Mammon'—had already been performed in Paris in 1880.[36] This was duly noted by the *Musical Times*, which nevertheless felt 'bound to accept the author's implied assurance that they are not identical'.[37]

After the concert, Widor wrote to Berger to thank the Society 'for the aimiable welcome and admirable performance'. With a stylish aristocratic gesture, he waived aside the payment of his expenses.[38] It was reported to the members that 'Widor, Tchaikovsky, Grieg and Svendsen had unanimously stated that the Society's band was the finest they had ever heard.'[39]

Another London concert was arranged at the beginning of 1890 on Widor's initiative. This time he offered Berger his new Fantaisie, Op. 62 for Piano and Orchestra, which had already been performed at the Concerts Colonne in 1889 with Isidor Philipp as soloist. Philipp, a distinguished pianist and, from 1893, a Professor at the Paris Conservatoire, was of Hungarian birth. He had first met Widor in 1886 and became one of his closest friends and champion of the Fantaisie and the two piano concertos.[40] Widor now proposed to bring him to London at his own expense.

In January 1890, Widor wrote to Berger: 'we confirm the date of the concert, March 13. It would seem to be more sound to rehearse the *Fantaisie*, once on the 12th., as it is very symphonic, but if there is no time, the 13th. will suffice.'[41] The players' phenomenal powers of sight-reading—which astonished Widor—were necessary to cope with the vast programme, including Mendelssohn's 'Scotch' Symphony and works by Weber, Mackenzie, Grétry, Bach, and Wagner.[42]

The Fantaisie is composed in a single movement, with a recurring and varied main theme. Particularly striking is the exhilarating three-part fugato in the strings against the soloist's independent flow of semiquavers. The piano writing is deft and sparkling, owing much to the concertos of Saint-Saëns. According to Philipp, the piece was particularly well received,[43] though the *Musical Times* made the false prediction that 'English amateurs are not likely to hear it again'.[44]

Later that year, in June, Widor scored a popular triumph at the Hippodrome at the Avenue de l'Alma in Paris with his ballet-pantomime *Jeanne d'Arc*, also described as a mimed legend. This was a well-trodden subject at the end of the century, to be raised to a nationalistic cult by the Catholic poet Charles Péguy. Widor's score, to a text by Dorchain, is laid out in four scenes for chorus and orchestra. Its musical style is unashamedly populist, even militaristic, with fanfares, marches, and big tunes. The opening pastoral scene at Domremy is interrupted by celestial voices—sung by two sopranos with harps—summoning Jeanne to her destiny. The action changes to the English camp at the siege of Orléans, with the chorus singing Charles d'Orléans's 'Le Temps a laissé son manteau'. After Jeanne is captured and brought to the stake, the pastoral theme and the celestial voices from Scene i reappear immediately before the moment of execution as a brief reminiscence—an effect surely inspired by Berlioz's 'March to the Scaffold'. In the final 'Apothéosis', an equestrian statue of Jeanne—sculpted by Frémiet—burst triumphantly from the flames! A rousing patriotic hymn 'Salut, O France des Aieux' ends the work. In a letter to Dorchain, Widor wrote:

'Thanks! But I'm becoming insatiable! I still need four verse-hexameters!'[45]

This patriotic spectacle presented various problems to overcome. The music had to take account of the Hippodrome's enormous spaces and echoes, for normally *cavalcades à grand fracas* were put on there.[46] During rehearsals, Widor became exhausted by having to cross the stale-smelling floor burning with the sun between the two orchestras 100 metres apart. Georges Clemenceau, the Radical politician and ardent patriot who liked to drop in on these preparations, advised him to take up smoking to combat the effects of the heat. In a newspaper interview at the end of his life, Widor recalled an amusing episode: 'They suggested to me a Roman chariot, the Duke of Brunswick's carriage, and finally a performing horse which bowed to the ladies. Clemenceau was most amused at my horsemanship. He came to see me every day and got me used to smoking cigarettes. I have continued to do so.'

After the final performance, Widor—who was delighted with the efforts of all involved[47]—received a plaster copy of Frémiet's statue of Jeanne d'Arc, which he kept proudly displayed on his piano.[48] Another award followed in October: in a letter from Cardinal Lavigerie, he learned that Pope Leo XIII had elevated him to be a Commander in the Order of Saint-Grégoire.[49] The following month, an unexpected event occurred which was to give his career a completely new turn.

6

THE ORGAN CLASS

ON 8 November, 1890 César Franck, the Organ Professor at the Paris Conservatoire, died as a result of a street accident in May that year. His funeral—attended by Widor and Guilmant, but not by the indisposed Director of the Conservatoire, Ambroise Thomas, who sent Delibes in his place—was the occasion for a fervent display of loyalty by his pupils. Chabrier gave the funeral oration: 'Farewell, master, and thank you, for you have done well!'[1]

Franck's death came as a bitter blow to his disciples in his class, which included two students of outstanding ability. Charles Tournemire had already completed his course at the Bordeaux Conservatoire, winning the First Prize for Piano at the age of 16. He continued his studies in Paris, joining Franck's class in October 1889. A close father-and-son relationship ensued, and one of the greatest experiences of his life was the occasion when Franck played through his newly composed *Trois Chorals* on the piano while his rapt pupil added the pedal part 'by hand'.[2]

Louis Vierne enrolled in October 1890, and was present for the four classes which the dying man succeeded in giving that month. Being partially-sighted, he had already sat at his feet at the Institut des Jeunes Aveugles.[3] Other members of that distinguished class were Henri Libert and Henri Busser. Sitting in as an observer was the future Bach scholar, André Pirro.

Now in reality this class was not exactly what it purported to be, for Franck neglected the teaching of playing technique and concentrated his energies on the improvisation side of the course. His overriding interest in bringing out the creative talents of his pupils can be seen as a manifestatation of a great composer's frustration at not obtaining a Professorship in Composition. Indeed, some composition students at the Conservatoire like d'Indy and Debussy had been drawn to Franck's class to experience for themselves his special methods and qualities.[4] In retrospect, a somewhat subversive situation had arisen. Within the august walls of the Conservatoire, here was a little state within a state, which, under the dominating leadership of d'Indy, was to grow into a powerful rival school of composition with the founding of the Schola Cantorum in 1894.

A characteristic lesson was later recalled by Tournemire. In response to Franck's direction to do 'something else' during the improvisation of a sonata-form movement, 'we pushed the swell pedal boisterously in our incapacity. We hoisted full sail and struck out according to our means! When danger arose, we were always rescued.'[5] In this charmed circle of devoted pupils, there was an atmosphere of apostolic intensity comparable to that of the Symbolist poet Mallarmé's 'Mardis'.

To fill the enormous void caused by Franck's death, Widor was approached by Thomas. But there were other names in the air with arguably greater claims to the post. Guilmant, the most senior, was perhaps the obvious choice. There was also Eugène Gigout, Professor at the Ecole Niedermeyer and organist of Saint-Augustin, and Henri Dallier, organist of Saint-Eustache.[6] All three had made their reputations primarily as organists, whereas Widor's musical activities were much more diversified. However, a factor which may well have weighed against Guilmant and Gigout was their close association with Franck, whom Thomas had openly reviled.[7]

As it happened, Widor hesitated. He was not by temperament an institutional type. An educator in the broad sense of widening students' horizons, he had a horror of examinations conditioning the content of courses and the utilitarian apparatus of student assessment. Nor did the status of a state functionary have any appeal. Rather, his independent and liberal spirit inclined him to favour the British system of self-governing Colleges of Music,[8] which he had witnessed in March that year, giving an organ recital at the Royal Academy of Music. Indeed, he had been toying with the idea of setting up his own private school of organ playing on the death of Franck.[9]

In the end, and after much thought, Widor accepted the professorship. (In accordance with procedure, the Director proposed three candidates: the Minister of Public Instruction traditionally chose the one who headed the list.[10]) Judging from a somewhat cryptic letter from Widor, there were powerful rumblings of discontent in the organ world: 'It seems that it is necessary to take seriously the furious attacks of the "blind man" as you say, alias Guilmant.' However, he added that he 'would be delighted to be of Delibes's clan at the Conservatoire'.[11]

At the same time, Widor had few illusions concerning the diplomatic problem facing him in his task of restoring the balance of the course's contents in the teeth of an apprehensive and latently hostile group of students. On 11 December he took over the class. He swept in and delivered an uncharacteristically formal set speech in which he outlined his aims and methods. Very careful not to antagonize the students by suggesting Franck's shortcomings, he acknowledged him as a brilliant improvisor; but he went on to say that 'in France, all too often performance is neglected for improvisation'. It was not enough to have ideas: improvisation 'could only be fully realised with the knowledge in depth and assiduous practice of all the resources offered by the manuals and pedals of the organ'. As for the interpretation of the works of J. S. Bach, it is necessary to possess a technique which 'is scientific and rational, not empirical'.[12]

A gruelling experience was in store, and, as Tournemire said to Vierne, 'It's clear, we know nothing.' To begin with, the atmosphere was glacial on both sides, but the intellectual force of Widor's presentation—using clearly formulated maxims and striking imagery—was irresistible. The best pupils found the courage and determination to cope with the enormous physical and mental reorientation which their teacher demanded. First, correct posture and economy of movement was vital: knees were to form a right angle with the thighs, and heels and knees were to be kept joined together as far as possible for security.

Much attention was paid to achieving a perfect legato and a precise staccato—the latter not cut too short for the sound to be inaudible. Organists, complained Widor, tend not to listen to themselves or take account of the acoustics, with the result that the musical texts remained unintelligible. He quoted Forkel that Bach 'observed with the most minute attention the acoustic properties of the room where he was to play'.[13] Articulation, punctuation, breathing, and accentuation were essential devices to provide the rhythmic dimension: 'Submit everything to the control of reason and express it with the will . . . through the force of will one gives the illusion of percussion'.[14] 'Would you like a

lesson in rhythm? Listen to those immense locomotives dragging
behind them tons of merchandise: admire the formidable piston
stroke which marks every recurrence of the accent, slowly but
relentlessly. Well may you believe that you hear the march of
Fate itself. It causes one to shudder.'[15]

Nothing should be left to chance. An organist should have an
architectural conception of performance in terms of straight lines
and designs.

By lines, when he passes slowly from *piano* into *forte* by a gradient
almost imperceptible and in constant progression without break or jolt.
By designs, when he takes advantage of a second of silence to close the
swell box abruptly between a *forte* and a *piano*. Seek to reproduce the
expressive quality of an E string or human voice, and we shall no longer
hear an organ; it will have become an accordion.[16]

Manual changes were to be made according to a precise and
intelligible organization of tone colour; Widor did not approve of
frequent changes of registration: 'No magic lanterns, if you
please.' Likewise, 'the passing from one tempo to another should
take place without disruption, and anticipated by a progressive
accelerando or ritardando regulated in a mathematically ordered
sequence of notes'.

The study of Bach formed an integral part of Widor's course.
He was ahead of his time in encouraging his pupils to take into
account the performing practices and instrumental limitations of
the eighteenth century when interpreting these works on modern
organs. Thus, heavy reeds were proscribed in most of the
preludes and fugues. Moderate and even rather slow tempi were
generally called for to preserve clarity of polyphonic textures, and
to avoid a mindlessly mechanical style in the allegro movements
of the trio sonatas and concertos.[17] 'Leave the speed record to the
taxi drivers!'[18] Widor was intelligently aware of the relativity of
time. After hearing a traditional style performance of a Haydn
symphony in Hungary, he wrote: 'Steam and electricity have
changed our way of life: all goes faster today. The notion of movement is modified in proportion. An *Allegro* now becomes a
Presto, an *Andante* an *Allegro*.'[19]

Whereas Franck had encouraged musical expressiveness in his
pupils' improvisations through melodic and harmonic invention,
Widor was primarily concerned with structure and logical

development. To this end, symphonies by C. P. E. Bach, Haydn, Mozart, Beethoven, Schubert, Mendelssohn, and Schumann were analysed, having been played to the class in piano duet versions. When he found his students incurious as to the way Beethoven had composed his sonatas, Widor exclaimed, 'that is the mentality of a parrot, not an artist'.

In due course, however, Widor was able to declare himself very satisfied with the progress of his class, and a genuinely friendly relationship was established. Nevertheless the Franckian ethos gave no sign of diminishing, but he showed no resentment when his students improvised in this style with bold chromatic harmonies: he confined himself to giving ingenious tips about thematic development. He could now go so far—without losing authority—as to admit that he had nothing fundamental to change in what Franck had taught them about improvisation.[20]

Although Tournemire was the most advanced player, it was the shy and docile Vierne who emerged as Widor's favourite pupil, and this feeling of admiration was mutual. Widor had the insight to perceive his potential genius, requiring time and care to come to fruition. Before long, he was giving Vierne private composition lessons free of charge, having persuaded him that to be a pure virtuoso would not satisfy his intellectual curiosity. Thus began his initiation into chamber music, symphonic writing, and orchestration.[21]

Tournemire and Vierne were indeed model students of enormous seriousness and dedication, but the severe disciplines of their studies could not dampen their natural gaiety and high spirits. Aided and abetted by their fellow student Henri Busser, they would even play jokes on Widor in class, as Tournemire has related. On one occasion, 'the great diapason kept permanently on the table in the organ room was sounded—at regular intervals—in such a way that Widor was convinced that there was a cornement to the 8' Bourdon on the second manual'. And Vierne had the idea 'of drawing the 16' Bassoon—and what a Bassoon—quite inappropriately, when our Professor called for a very soft bass to balance the Gamba and Voix Celeste'. When Widor once was called away from his class, Tournemire 'set his classmates dancing to the sounds of an incredible musical shindy' until he was thrown out by the irate Secretary of the Conservatoire.[22]

In the competition of 1891, in which all the students played
works by Bach, Tournemire gained the First Prize, but
ominously—as the future was to reveal—no Second Prize was
awarded.[23] At this point, he left the class to become Widor's
assistant at Saint-Sulpice. In February 1892 however, he moved
on to become organist of Saint-Médard,[24] eventually succeeding
Pierné at Franck's old church of Sainte-Clotilde, where he
established his reputation as an incomparable improvisor. For a
few years he seems to have maintained some contact with Widor,
dedicating his motet 'Pater Noster', Op. 8 (1894) 'to my dear
master Ch-M. Widor'. Two very early organ pieces—the
Andantino Op. 2 and *Sortie* Op. 3—were published along with
others by Vierne and Libert in the series *l'Orgue moderne*, which
Widor founded and edited.[25] But the memory of Franck was too
potent, the identification too complete for him to form any other
really close relationship. In any case, to this idealistic youth, a
devout Catholic of mystical tendencies, Widor's style of life may
have seemed too worldly and hedonistic. Tournemire ploughed
his own lonely furrow towards the supreme achievement of
the *l'Orgue mystique* following Franck's advice: 'Discover
yourself—it will take years.' [26]

After Tournemire's departure, Vierne soon became a marked
man and was entrusted with a subsidiary course in plainchant
accompaniment and fugal improvisation, which Widor introduced for those observers who intended to become full members
of the class. This course was held in Alkan's old study in Erard's
studios.[27] Four months later, Vierne succeeded Tournemire as
assistant at Saint-Sulpice. The colossal instrument filled him with
alarm; but Widor reassured him: 'I will only leave you in the big
bath when you have learned to swim.' He eased his nervous pupil
into the position by sitting beside him on the organ stool, and
soon he could tackle an entire service singlehanded.[28]

Vierne still remained a member of the organ class and com-
peted for the First Prize in July 1892, playing Franck's *Grande
Pièce Symphonique*. The previous year, Widor had been criticized
by the jury for not including any of his predecessor's works in the
programme, but now he refused to countenance any cuts to the
Grande Pièce, even though its length would infringe the rules.[29]
In the competition Vierne played outstandingly well on the
notoriously inadequate organ of the Conservatoire, but to the

general amazement he gained only a Second Prize; no First Prize was awarded. Widor became very pale and bore off his star pupil in his arms, consoling him with the fact that he had never won any prizes. The other students reacted by hurling insults at the jury and its chairman Theodore Dubois, Professor of Composition, who was standing in for the indisposed Director, Thomas.[30]

Later, one of the jury members, Emile Bernard joined Widor at an indignant meeting with his students at a restaurant. Bernard revealed that three of them—Guilmant, Dallier, and himself—had voted a First Prize for Vierne, but the others had made vague criticisms of the excessive length of the *Grande Pièce*, and the harshness of his harmonies in the improvisation. 'Thank you', replied Widor; 'I despise this bunch of failures, and you can tell them so from me . . . when I am in a position to repay them, they may be sure that I shan't miss the chance'.[31]

What were their motives?- It might be charitable to suppose that Pierné (Franck's pupil and successor at Sainte-Clotilde), Gigout (who played at Franck's funeral), and Dubois (who recommended Franck to Thomas for the Organ Professorship in 1872) were jealously guarding the sacred memory of their 'Pater Seraphicus'. The other men—Raoul Pugno, Henri Fissot, Theodore Salomé, and Emile Réty[32]—were more obviously acting from spite, for as Philipp tells us, 'other artists envying Widor's position in the world, angry because he lived retired and independent, agitated against him'.[33] Later competitions were to reveal a conspiracy to deny First Prizes to Widor's pupils. Admittedly, substantially the same jury had given Tournemire this prize, but his prowess was doubtlessly attributable—in their eyes—to his year with Franck; whereas Vierne had come almost entirely under Widor's formative influence. (Happily, in later years, Pierné, Dubois, and Pugno were to revise their opinion of Widor.)

But whatever their reasons, the result was capable of being interpreted as a serious vote of no confidence in the new Professor. By the irony of circumstances, the outstanding prize-winner, as it were, at the Conservatoire's prize-giving ceremony the following month, was Widor himself. The Cross of the Legion of Honour was presented to him by the Minister for the Fine Arts.[34]

The stresses of that year took their toll on Widor's usually excellent health. In March, the Conservatoire had received a telegram: 'Excuse me from my class at the Conservatoire tomorrow: suffering from asphyxia last night.' In September, he was convalescing in Persannes l'Arbresle par Rhone; but the heat—'like the burning Sirocco'—was too much for him.[35] The following January, he travelled to Budapest to conduct a concert, but there he complained of the 26 degrees of cold: 'The Danube resembles a sea of marble—it is frozen over. The rehearsal went well, an excellent orchestra. Yesterday, the wine in the restaurant-car was half frozen.'[36]

Increasingly, Widor was becoming a father-figure to Vierne, who was persuaded to continue in the organ class and with his composition lessons. Their scope increased as he matured, embracing in addition a broad field of historical and musicological studies. His teacher was also concerned with his general education, encouraging him to acquaint himself with Latin and Greek, French literature, and History of Art: 'I cannot understand an ignorant musician. Everything which belongs to the intellectual world is intimately bound up: music has definite connections with painting, sculpture, literature, and even the exact sciences, mathematics, geometry, algebra and acoustics.'

Widor was convinced that Vierne was above all destined to be a composer. 'Wouldn't you be tempted to write beautiful Organ Symphonies, for example? They would benefit from your aesthetic created by Franck, and the discoveries which I have sown in my Eight Symphonies.'[37] Over the next three decades, this suggestion bore magnificent fruit in Vierne's six symphonies, based, like Widor's, on a rising scale of tonalities. It is highly significant that neither Tournemire nor Vierne attended the operatically oriented composition classes at the Conservatoire; but it is more surprising that neither of them appear to have turned to d'Indy for lessons.[38]

In the following year's Competition, a similar disturbing verdict was passed on Widor and his students. The jury, chaired by Thomas, again awarded no First Prize, and even declined to re-award the Second Prize to Vierne, which went instead to Achille Runner. Vierne had been given a warm reception by the audience for his performance of Bach's Passacaglia and Fugue in C minor, BWV 582, and Widor, in a towering rage, condemned the whole proceedings as a lottery. His disciple merely shrugged his shoulders with disdain, vowing to have another 'stab' next year.[39]

Plate 1 Charles-Marie Widor

Plate 2 Widor on the shores of Lake Geneva

Plate 3 Marcel Dupré at the West door of Saint-Sulpice, 1961

Plate 4 Widor at the organ of Saint-Sulpice

In the end, such courage and persistence was rewarded, and in July 1894, he finally gained his First Prize shared with Libert, the future organist of Saint-Denis. Vierne had almost set out to antagonize the jury in his improvisation with bold strokes which delighted the audience. At long last, Thomas had got wind of the conspiracy, and threatened to nullify the decision if necessary.[40] Afterwards, Guilmant congratulated Vierne on his magisterial performance of Bach's Prelude and Fugue in B minor, BWV 544.

To celebrate this crowning achievement, Widor arranged a party at the Restaurant Durand, in which he gave way to his sense of mischief. In addition to Vierne, the guests consisted of Libert, Dallier, Bernard, Guilmant, Pugno, Carolus Duran, Imbert, Forain—and Dubois. The last-named, very prim and proper, fell headlong into the trap which Widor had prepared, as a small return for his chairmanship of the jury of 1892.

As prearranged, Dubois's glass was kept well topped up throughout the evening. Knowing his man, Widor waited his moment and came out with a risqué joke. The upright moralist—who was later to forbid his students to attend the performances of Debussy's *Pelléas et Mélisande*[41]—proceeded to regale the company with highly dubious stories about former female pupils, describing their charms in unrestrained detail. Egged on by Widor and Dallier, his performance culminated in a recital of obscene songs 'which would make a fireman blush'. This episode soon became the talk of the artistic world of Paris, and earned Dubois the reputation of a comedian. Widor had had the last laugh.[42]

MUSICAL CHAIRS

WIDOR'S devotion to duty as Professor of Organ did not signal a retreat from the world. He conducted the première of his Symphonie No. 3, Op. 69 for orchestra and organ solo, which took place in November 1894 at the inauguration of the Victoria Hall, Geneva. This work is indebted to the corresponding symphonie of Saint-Saëns in its structural division into two large distinct movements, reuniting the four movements in groups of two. A choral-type theme plays an important part throughout. Vierne, who took the solo part, was plagued by nerves, brought on both by the problematic nature of the newly installed Cavaillé-Coll organ and by the vagaries of Widor's conducting 'of which it was sometimes difficult to have an absolute certitude', as his loyal disciple admitted.[1]

Nevertheless, Widor felt able to write to Imbert that the performance was 'a great success beyond all hopes—the German party was the first to shout Bravo!'[2] The following incident also bears out the view that his music is more German than French in character. When the Berlin Philharmonic Orchestra under Nikisch visited Paris in May 1898, three young cyclists in the audience protested at the inclusion of the *Conte d'avril* Suite in the programme, exclaiming that 'one doesn't play Widor after Beethoven'. To which a voice from the First Violins replied: 'That's not French music.'[3]

In March 1896, Thomas died, and Dubois succeeded him as Director of the Conservatoire for an initial period of five years, and with considerably reduced powers regarding the appointment of staff and the admission of students. Widor applied successfully to take Dubois's place as one of the three Professors of Composition, although he felt a keen sadness at leaving his organ students.[4] As it happened, Massenet resigned in October, and it was now Fauré's turn to enter the portals of the Conservatoire as junior Composition Professor. The newly created 'Conseil

Superieure' obviously realized the urgent need for new blood, as the Schola Cantorum had just opened its doors as a teaching establishment: neither Widor or Fauré were Conservatoire products or Prix de Rome winners, unlike Dubois and the senior Professor, Charles Lenepveu. However, it was Lenepveu who triumphed over Widor and Fauré in the election to Thomas's chair at the highly conservative Institut de France that year.[5]

Widor's immediate problem was to manœuvre a worthy successor into place in the Organ Class, and to safeguard Vierne's position as assistant. He played his political contacts, and in December introduced Guilmant to his new students in an atmosphere of mutual congratulations. Widor was determined to maintain contact with his former class, and, over lunch at Foyot's, Vierne would keep him informed as to its progress. Guilmant proved to be a Professor of the highest distinction, and Vierne became devoted to him.[6]

Vierne, however, remained mystified as to why Widor had wanted to become a Professor of Composition: 'did he think he would have as positive an influence as that which he had acquired in the organ class by the personality of his teaching, and enlarge the horizons of young composers . . . I do not know whether the future left him that illusion'.[7] The basic problem lay in the time-honoured methods of the composition classes, which—under a line of professors including Delibes, Massenet, and Thomas—concentrated exclusively on the techniques of operatic writing; indeed, the composer of *Mignon* had firmly rejected a plea for the introduction of instrumental composition: 'No musician of standing would condescend to become a mere teacher of symphonie.'[8] In Calvocoressi's account, 'many things of Beethoven, too, were thought to set a bad example; and Wagner's music, naturally, even more so'.[9] It was the Schola Cantorum which was destined to become the forcing-house of the post-Franckian school of symphonists, d'Indy and his pupils Magnard and Roussel.

Neither Widor nor Fauré could discard this legacy of the past, since an operatic-based training was necessary if the students were to compete for the Prix de Rome, a valuable award which entitled the winner to four years' residence at the Villa Medici in Rome. According to its anachronistic rules and procedures, the competitors were incarcerated in single rooms in the Château de

Compiègne to compose the obligatory cantata on a given text, together with a vocal fugue. The finalists conducted performances of their cantatas at the Institut de France, to be judged by all the members of the Académie des Beaux-Arts.

Inevitably, the pedestrian Lenepveu, who knew the ropes, was the most successful teacher for the Prix de Rome. Nevertheless, it was Fauré—who concentrated on chamber music and was sympathetic to the Symbolist movement—who at first attracted most of the truly creative spirits like Ravel, Florent Schmitt, Roger-Ducasse, and Nadia Boulanger. Yet he had fewer Prix de Rome winners than Widor, who possessed considerable experience of writing operas. Vierne tells us that Widor 'would occasionally try to make his students write symphonic music, but most of his time was taken up with the cookery of the Cantata'. [10]

Widor, however, managed to overcome these limitations to a considerable extent over the years, for his classes produced not a school but a wealth of individual creative personalities. 'He displayed', wrote Marcel Dupré, 'a great breadth of mind in attempting to penetrate the temperament of each one and guide it in its own path. Always straightforward and kindly towards his pupils, he had, beneath a certain outward coldness, a warmth of heart which revealed a deep sensitiveness.' [11]

His concern was not confined to the classroom. One of his first pupils, Gabriel Dupont, distinguished himself by making an appearance in the police court while competing for the Prix de Rome. During the night he had escaped from the Château and broken some glass while sliding down a drainpipe, all to gather roses for 'some charming girls who came under our windows to listen to the valses which we played for them after dinner'. Widor was able to arrange his release, [12] and the amorous youth went on to produce works of distinction; *Antar* was regarded by Prunières as 'the best modern opera produced in France since *Samson et Delila*'.

As the century ended, Cavaillé-Coll reached the end of his life on 13 October 1899. A poor businessman, his last years had been clouded with serious financial problems, as he had priced himself out of the market by refusing to compromise his exemplary standards of craftsmanship and materials. [13] When Widor asked Ferry for help on his behalf, the seasoned barrister replied:

Musicians are charming dreamers. Where do you think I can find 50,000 francs for the worthy Cavaillé-Coll . . . the hole must be much deeper. Never has the Commercial Court made such an honest man bankrupt for 50,000 francs. Without doubt, it is not the bankruptcy but the liquidation which threatens him. That's all, my dear friend. I can do absolutely nothing.[14]

In the end, the firm was saved and taken over by Charles Mutin, but Cavaillé-Coll died a poor man. Albert Schweitzer remembered him as a regular visitor to the organ loft at Saint-Sulpice 'with his little cap and with his good true eyes in which so much of art and intelligence lay. He would sit on the organ stool and run his hands over the console of his.'[15] Widor played the organ for his well-attended funeral at Saint-Sulpice.[16]

As one door closed, another opened. In 1900, Sergent, the organist of Notre Dame, died, and Widor pressed Vierne to enter the gruelling competition for a successor. Notre Dame, however, being a poor parish, offered only a small salary and as a newly married man, pressure was exerted on him to apply for the wealthy church of Saint-Pierre de Neuilly. But for Widor, the path was clear: the glory of the cathedral of Paris should be his sole consideration. These counsels prevailed, and Vierne was unanimously chosen by the selection committee—chaired by Widor—among which were the familiar faces of Fauré, Guilmant, Gigout, Dallier, and Dubois.[17] Like Widor at Saint-Sulpice, he was inspired by the building, the traditions, and the great services of the cathedral.[18]

Over the next few years, Widor was occupied with a project of a very different nature, the fruits of his experience as a composer of orchestral music. His *Technique de l'orchestre moderne*—conceived as a supplement to Berlioz's celebrated treatise—appeared in 1904, and was very influential. Stravinsky possessed a copy, and Ravel—whose teacher Fauré was little interested in this subject—constantly referred to it.[19] He took great care over each separate block of woodwind, brass, and strings, following Widor's precept: 'Write orchestral music so that each group can be heard without the others.'

Widor shows himself extremely sensitive to the sound proper-ties of instruments. Very practical, he is always conscious of their capacities for blending with each other, and of the weak parts of their registers. Lists of shakes, tremolos, and multiple stoppings are set out with a Germanic thoroughness, in consultation with leading professors and bandmasters. Yet he wears his learning lightly, and the book is a joy to read: it stimulates the aural imagination as a good cookery book the palate.

The discoveries of acoustics provide a scientific foundation. 'Nothing should be written which is not in keeping with the nature of the instrument.' He deplores the tendency of young composers to write high trumpet parts: 'The real trumpet begins with Haydn and Mozart, the imperious and manly trumpet of Beethoven, Weber, Wagner and Berlioz, neither too high or too low.' Glissandi on pedal timpani—later used with such poetry by Bartók—are remarked on as a curious effect; 'Is it really the Drum's function to run up and down rapid scales?'

If in some ways the book is backward-looking, in others it looks to the future. Widor has little patience with archaic notations and procedures, condemning the absurdity of horn transpositions and the problem of the G clef for the cello. Likewise, he is forward-looking in his attention to the percussion, and in his awareness of its poetic potential. When the cymbal is hit with a soft stick, 'a cloud of gold-dust seems to rise out of the orchestra'. The musical quotations range widely through the scores of the Classical and Romantic eras. There is even a short harp extract from Debussy's *Pelléas et Mélisande*, first performed two years before.

Meanwhile, compositions continued to flow. As well as two more magnificent organ symphonies (to be discussed in the next chapter), Widor's output in these years included the Piano Concerto No. 2, Op. 77, the Violin Sonata No. 2, Op. 79, and the Symphonie Antique (1911) with a choral Finale based on the 'Te Deum'.

1905 could be called the French 'Year of the Sea', for, besides Debussy's *La Mer*, there appeared Widor's opera *Les Pêcheurs de Saint-Jean*, subtitled 'Scènes de la vie maritime'. It was produced at the Opéra Comique in December by Albert Carré, who had taken the brave decision a few years earlier to put on *Pelléas et Mélisande*. Widor's opera, in four Acts with a libretto by Henri Cain, portrays the lives of simple fisherfolk; the elemental force of the sea is depicted by a stark theme for trombones, used previously in the 'Apotheosis' scene of *Jeanne d'Arc*. As well as the generally simplified textures and folk-style themes, the score is remarkable for the faithful reproduction of conversational speech in the vocal lines, inspired by the fluid recitative writing of *Pelléas*.

Les Pêcheurs was greeted with considerable acclaim, yet, if Phillipp is to be believed, it fell a victim to intrigue:

Unfortunately, Widor had chosen for the chief role a remarkable singer [Claire Friché] for whom Marguerite Carré, the all-powerful wife of the Director, harboured a deep dislike. She had wished to have the role for herself, but the inflexible Widor did not want to take it away from the interpreter he had himself chosen. Carré, ruled by his wife, did everything he could to cause the opera to be retired from the repertoire.[20]

Amid the continual intrigue of musical politics, Widor remained in a state of neutrality, maintaining his friendships with Massenet and Saint-Saëns of the Institut party, and—very daringly for a Conservatoire professor—showing himself sympathetic both to Franck's school (for all its uncongenial dogmatism) and to Debussy, anathematized as they were by the cultural establishment. Widor admired the formidable powers of organization and pedagogy possessed by d'Indy, who had assumed the Directorship of the Schola Cantorum in 1900—but with the qualification: 'What a pity that such a man is not musical!'[21]

In 1903 Widor stood boldly alongside d'Indy, Debussy, Ravel, Caplet, Vidal, and Chaminade in a joint invitation by Paul Gravolet, a member of the Comédie Française, to set one poem each from his *Frissons*. Widor's setting is lost, although Debussy's 'Dans le jardin' and Ravel's 'Manteau de fleurs' have survived.[22] Six years later, Widor joined Debussy, Ravel, d'Indy, Dukas, and Hahn to contribute a piano piece to the *Review SIM* to mark the anniversary of the death of Haydn. Saint-Saëns and Fauré declined to take part.[23]

However, in this epoch of rapid scientific and cultural change, it was inevitable that Widor's works as a whole began to appear somewhat dated in the face of the meteoric rise of the Impressionists, and modernists like Richard Strauss and Skryabin. After a concert in the Queen's Hall, London in May 1909, in which Widor conducted the Symphonie No. 3, the Fantaisie and *Bacchanale*, the *Musical Times* commented that 'his refusal or inability to fall into line with modern vagaries has deprived him of due recognition as a composer in all forms'.[24] But from the vantage point of the late twentieth century, it is possible to describe him as a creative conservative, grafting the most enduring aspects of the new onto the older traditions.

Meanwhile, in 1905, a storm had broken over the Conservatoire and the Institut: Ravel's failure in the Prix de Rome caused a public outcry. This miniature Dreyfus case of the musical world forced Dubois, as representative of the system, to resign the Directorship, and Fauré—who possessed the necessary experience as Inspector of the Provincial Conservatoires—was appointed in his place, with instructions to implement a radical seven-point reform plan. *Inter alia*, this provided that the Composition Professors were to be relieved of their task of teaching counterpoint, although fugue remained within their province. The Conservatoire's teaching of these disciplines had for long been weak,[25] but Widor and the new Professor of Counterpoint, André Gedalge, were formidably equipped to rectify this state of affairs.

Despite the rival pull of the Schola Cantorum, the Conservatoire continued to attract aspiring young composers, some of whom were to become leaders of the post-war modern movements. Darius Milhaud and Arthur Honegger joined Widor's fugue class in 1907. In 1915, Milhaud, exempted from active military service, entered Widor's composition class[26] before leaving to assist Paul Claudel, the French Consul in Rio de Janeiro. Milhaud had already formed his own distinctive harmonic style in an impressive list of compositions for a student, including the song-cycle *Alissa* and an opera *La Brebis Egarée*. Of Widor he wrote: 'That charming teacher, a most brilliant conversationalist, would utter cries of alarm at every dissonance he came across in my works; as he listened, he would exclaim: "the worst of it is that you get used to them!" How far away the justifiably severe criticisms that Gedalge used to make!'[27]

Ironically, the most revolutionary of Widor's pupils, Edgard Varèse, was particularly appreciative of him, having joined his composition class in 1906, after leaving the Schola. In comparison with d'Indy, Widor was 'human, unpretentious, open-minded and had a sense of humour . . . Roussel, Widor, Massenet and Debussy might represent an élite of France, but the bourgeois majority in Paris were personified . . . by d'Indy, Saint-Saëns and Fauré, [who] kept music static, stayed the imagination and stopped the flow of life'.[28] This tribute is all the more impressive as coming from a man who went on to study with Busoni and Strauss; it was Widor's profound knowledge of the Austro-German tradition, and of the orchestra which Varèse valued especially.

Nadia Boulanger and Marcel Dupré were more conventional. Boulanger, who became a great teacher in her own right, had already gained a First Prize in Fauré's class in 1905, before joining Widor's unofficially, on Pugno's advice. Fauré, not unnaturally, was hurt, and this can only have further soured relationships between him and Widor. Her attempt at the Prix de Rome in 1907 was unsuccessful. In a letter of commiseration, her teacher offered some helpful advice: 'Your technique is superior to that of the other candidates . . . unfortunately, the effect was greatly diminished in the Great Hall of the Institut . . . You should work on the exterior, decorative element next year.'

Complying with regulations seems to have presented something of a problem to Widor's pupils. At her attempt in 1908, Boulanger scandalized the musical world by submitting an instrumental fugue instead of the prescribed vocal one. Demands for her disqualification were led by Saint-Saëns, who disapproved of women composers. Finally, the Minister for the Fine Arts ruled in her favour, as she pleaded ignorance of the rules, and submitted that the character of the given fugue subject was more suited to instruments. In the final round, she was awarded the Second Prize, consisting of a gold medal.[29]

Dupré entered Widor's composition class in 1908. Two years before, he had become his assistant at Saint-Sulpice while still a pupil of Guilmant: as had been the case with Vierne, he had not yet gained his First Prize for Organ, and voices were again raised in protest. A close relationship grew up between him and Widor, who came to regard him as his new spiritual son in place of Vierne, who was becoming increasingly withdrawn through illness and domestic crises.

Dupré, with his great facility in counterpoint, won the First Prize for Fugue, beating Milhaud and Honegger, and five years later, in 1914, the Prix de Rome. The outbreak of war prevented him from taking up residence at the Villa Medici; in 1916, he became acting organist of Notre Dame while Vierne was convalescing in Switzerland. At the end of hostilities, Widor forbade him to go to Rome: 'You cannot abandon Notre Dame, or dream away four years at the Villa Medici . . . you are 33 . . . it is time to begin your career'.[30]

For all his success as a celebrity recitalist, Dupré remained Widor's assistant at Saint-Sulpice (apart from the period at Notre Dame) until the latter's retirement in 1933. It became the custom for Dupré to play during the Offertoire: on the spur of the moment, Widor would request a piece—usually by Bach—which Dupré proceeded to play from memory! His incomparable mastery of the organ led him to compose a series of showpieces, but amongst his compositions some of a higher inspiration stand out, notably the magnificent *Symphonie-Passion*, Op. 23.

While his students were busy competing, Widor continued his ascent towards the Institut de France, having already been made a Corresponding Member of the Académies of Berlin (1906), Belgium (1907), and Stockholm (1909). A vacancy in the Académie des Beaux-Arts occurred in 1909, but this time he was defeated by Fauré, who benefited from the support of his father-in-law, the sculptor Frémiet, and from Saint-Saëns.[31] Success, however, crowned Widor's attempt the following year.

In March 1911, Guilmant died. Widor had set his heart on Vierne to succeed him as Professor of Organ at the Conservatoire. The organist of Notre Dame was now of a sufficient age, standing, and experience to be promoted. Fauré, however, wished to nominate Gigout who had been his fellow student at the Ecole Niedermeyer. According to Vierne, Widor brought the issue to a head by undiplomatically attacking Fauré in front of mutual friends: the Director, on hearing of this, took offence and enlisted Saint-Saëns's help in persuading the reluctant Gigout to stand, as an act of retaliation.[32]

Gigout's appointment was a bitter blow. But in reality, it was Widor's pride rather than his school which suffered, for he and Guilmant were not, as they fondly believed, the sole fountainhead of authentic Bach performance in France. Loret, Gigout's teacher, had also studied with Lemmens, and his tradition thus flowed on through the Ecole Niedermeyer—albeit rather more quietly. By Vierne's own admission, Gigout was one of the few—apart from Franck, Widor, Guilmant, and Saint-Saëns—who was aware of the existence of Bach's chorale preludes. When Widor's pupils had played them in the 1892 examinations, Thomas exclaimed: 'Why did I not know about this forty years ago?'[33]

From Widor's standpoint, all was not lost, for the Organ Professorship at the Schola Cantorum had also become vacant on Guilmant's death: d'Indy proceeded to appoint Vierne to the post. At least Widor could see his tradition continuing at the Schola.

8

CATHOLICISM AND PROTESTANTISM

THE events of the previous chapter, with Widor pursuing his ambitions and helping his pupils to realize theirs, would, on their own, give a misleading account of his life during these years. In contact with leading politicians and literary figures as he was, he would have been fully aware of the sombre intellectual climate setting in at the end of the century. Disillusionment with the ideals of the Third Republic—Positivism, faith in scientific discovery, egalitarianism—led two of his old friends to seek their salvation both in the arms of the Catholic Church and in authoritarian nationalistic political movements: Bourget joined Maurras's *Action Française*, and Coppée the *Ligue de la Patrie Française*, of which Barrès was among the founders.

The Church and the Republic remained at loggerheads in spite of attempts by Pope Leo XIII, Cardinal Lavigerie, and Widor's friend Etienne Lamy to lead a *ralliement*, by which the church would work to unite Liberals and Catholics. However, these hopes of co-operating with the Republic were sabotaged by the parish priests with their Royalist sympathies. Mutual hostilities culminated in the separation of church and state in 1906.[1]

Under Briand's law of separation, the state no longer supported the church. Inventories of church property began to be taken by fiscal inspectors, which were in some cases stoutly resisted. At Sainte-Clotilde, where Tournemire was organist, the Royalist congregation, with the support of the *Action Française*, provoked a full-scale siege by police and firemen, and nearly 300 defenders were arrested or seriously injured.[2]

Choir schools were badly affected by this new situation and many organists had their salaries cut by a quarter. Organ building also stagnated.[3] But fabric above all was in danger. Churches throughout France were being demolished for lack of means to maintain them. In 1911, Barrès organized a successful petition to the Parliament for their protection similar to that granted to historic monuments, and a vast number of creative artists and almost the entire Institut de France came to his support.[4]

This national concern for its church buildings—as opposed to the political pretensions of the clergy—reflects the healthier aspect of the conservative reaction which gripped large sections of the country. Independent as ever, Widor refused to be drawn towards any partisan position. It is noticeable, however, that with middle age, he looked increasingly to institutions as a support and to give meaning to life. Like his influential cousin Bourget—who claimed to speak for his generation—he may well have found his sense of individualism too painful to sustain.[5] His loyalty to Saint-Sulpice, devotion to his students, and enthusiastic membership of the Institut point to this. A delight in historical continuities—as with his tradition of organ playing stretching back in an unbroken line to Bach himself—was allied with a proper sense of national pride, manifest in his lengthy campaign for the restoration of the organ in Saint-Louis des Invalides.[6] He remained too much of an internationalist in outlook to subscribe to the anti-German chauvinism of Maurras and Barrès, who agitated for the return of Alsace-Lorraine to France.

The Catholic reaction also brought about a revival of the cultural and intellectual foundations of the church. In 1879, the theology of Saint Thomas Aquinas was pronounced official by Leo XIII; the monks of Solesmes made exhaustive researches into the sources of plainchant; and the Schola Cantorum was founded in 1894 primarily for the study of early church music. Composers began to make use of plainchant in their own works: Guilmant in his *l'Orgue liturgiste*, Op. 65 (1884), and Gigout in his *Album Gregorien* (1895).

Widor's own intensive use of plainchant at this time as a major source of inspiration and musical material—both in his liturgical improvisations and in his last two organ symphonies—surely testifies to the deepening of his religious faith. In these works, he employed his chosen plainchant themes according to the cyclic principle of Franck and his school, as a unifying factor in a multitude of transformations; the earlier ethos of secular humanism now gave way to a spiritual inwardness and sense of mystery. As their titles and dedications suggest, the Symphonie 'Gothique' and the Symphonie 'Romane' point in opposite geographical directions: the former to the North, with its rugged counterpoint and deliberate archaism; the latter to the South, with its more open luminous textures and serene Italianate atmosphere.

The Symphonie 'Gothique' in C minor, Op. 70 (1895) is dedicated to the church of Saint-Ouen, Rouen, with an invocation of its patron saint: 'Ad memoriam Sancti Andoeni Rothomagensis'. This church's celebrated Cavaillé-Coll organ had been inaugurated by Widor in 1890; the *titulaire* was Albert Dupré, father of Marcel.[7] The 'Gothique' is really an extraordinary conception. Its four movements are highly contrasted with something of the eclecticism of the Op. 13 set.

The Moderato's tormented, anguished character—arising from the extended chromatic and appoggiatura-laden melodic lines clashing together within the closely worked polyphony—anticipates the mature style of Vierne, who gave its première at the Eglise d'Ecully, Lyon.[8] This hyper-expressive material, however, is contained within a tight Baroque structure with heavy sequential writing and a relentless flow of even quavers. In Widor's own recording (1932), this rigidity is mitigated by a judicious use of rubato and a sense of the 'grandes lignes'.

The Sulpician calm of the Andante sostenuto comes as a welcome contrast. A slowly unfolding melody is given an almost orchestral breadth of treatment, with double-pedal parts adding to the textural richness. The movement ends in a shimmering haze of added second and sixth harmonies. The Gothic world returns in the Allegro, a fully worked-out fugue, in which the plainchant for the Feast of Christmas, 'Puer natus est' emerges for the first time as an independent pedal part, in powerful augmentation.

In the final Moderato, Widor in effect pays homage to Guilmant with a *tour de force* consisting of a journey through the history of organ music from the sixteenth to the nineteenth century, surely inspired by the latter's recitals at the Trocadéro. In a series of skilful pastiches, the 'Puer natus est' theme first appears in a breathtakingly beautiful modal harmonization; as a cantus firmus in a contrapuntal texture; and in strict canons at the octave. After this formidable demonstration of academic expertise, the movement concludes with a 'Toccata' in Widor's own authentic style, culminating in a climax of incandescent power.

The Symphonie 'Romane' in D major, Op. 73 (1900) is again dedicated to a church and its saint, here to Saint-Sernin,

Toulouse, with the inscription 'Ad memoriam Sancti Saturnini Tolosensis'. The plainchant for Easter Day, 'Haec dies', plays a fundamental role in all the movements, apart from the penultimate 'Cantabile'. Indeed, the chant is extensively worked, being the source of virtually all their melodic material; but such were Widor's powers of variation and development that there is no sense of monotony.

The essentially repetitive nature of the 'Haec dies' plainchant is reflected in the overall style of the symphonie. The predominant rate of harmonic change is very slow—with long stretches of D and F major harmonies and massive pedal-points—and much brilliant Lisztian figuration is effectively employed to fill these expanses of musical space. Immobility and stasis, however, are cunningly avoided with contrasting chromatic sections and sudden leaps into remote key areas. Ostinato patterns, found in the Moderato, 'Choral', and 'Final', provide both the slow march rhythms in the pedals and the gentle rocking motions which invest this work with a wonderful tenderness and grace.

By a masterstroke, the remarkable passage which opens the symphonie—the chant stated in free rhythm against a background of arabesques and pedal-points—is recapitulated in the coda of the 'Final'. Both this and the exhilarating plainchant fantasia section in the 'Final' uncannily look ahead to the monumental l'Orgue mystique of Tournemire.

The performance of the 'Romane' seems to have caused Widor considerable birthpangs. His pupil, Albert Schweitzer

stood beside [him] while studying [it] and how many times he returned to certain places before couplers and combination pedals obeyed him as he wished . . . one May Sunday, Widor, still striving with technical problems, played for the first time in Saint-Sulpice the *Romane*. I felt with him that in this work, the French art of organ playing had entered sacred art, and had experienced that death and that resurrection that every art of organ playing must experience when it wishes to create something new.[9]

Widor was also deeply concerned with plainchant in the context of public worship. He had strong views on the subject of the researches of the monks of Solesmes, who had published primary manuscript sources of plainchant in their *Paléographie Musicale* (1888). This became the groundwork for the commission set up in 1904 by Pope Pius X, to prepare the *Editio*

Vaticana, a new official edition of the chant books. Great was the general astonishment that there was no place on it for musicians of the eminence of Widor, Saint-Saëns, Dubois, Paladilhe, or Gevaert.[10]

This did not prevent Widor from addressing a paper to Baron Kanzler at the Vatican in robust terms. He praised the monks for reproducing 'a colossal monument', but took them to task for their uncritical presentation of all the source material, good and bad, true and false. He went on to assert the superiority of the older syllabic hymns like the ancient 'Lauda Sion'; 'beautiful lines' as opposed to the decadence of melismata and vocalises with 'too many ornaments, too many accents, too many notes'. On the practical level, he maintained that the complexities of melismatic chant, the revival of archaic neumatic notation and the application of the monks' rhythmic theories were unsuitable for the average parish. Here he seems to speak with the voice of Ferry in a plea for *sociability*: 'Must we have two Antiphonaries, one for wealthy choirs, the other for poor churches?'[11]

The books of the *Editio Vaticana* began to appear from 1905, and the results were as Widor feared. Controversy raged around both it and the practical implications of the Pope's *Motu proprio* of 1903 which sanctioned the work of the Schola Cantorum by prescribing the almost exclusive use of plainchant and sixteenth-century polyphony in the services, admitting only those modern compositions that contained nothing profane or theatrical. As Saint-Saëns sagely observed, 'it was a total overthrow of secular habits'.[12] During an audience subsequently granted to Widor in 1909, Pius X unburdened himself: 'What was my wish? To separate the music of the church from the music of the theatre, and put a little order into the ecclesiastical chant.' He complained about 'the ideological sectarianism attributed to him, the anarchic disorder of those congresses which multiply in exact proportion to their uselessness . . . Nobody listens to me!'[13]

Equally unsatisfactory were Widor's other dealings with the Vatican. It had been Cavaillé-Coll's dream to build an organ for Saint Peter's, Rome, one more befitting the centre of Christendom than the existing small instrument mounted on wheels. The project, initially well received by Pius IX and Leo XIII, was lost in the maze of curial bureaucracy and the indifference of the Roman public. It was revived under the Pontificate of Pius X for com-

pletion by Cavaillé's successor, Mutin, with a fund raising committee set up under Widor's chairmanship. The meagre sum of
60,000 francs eventually raised was allocated instead to the
paving of the choir.[14]

Meanwhile, after he had ceased to be Professor of Organ,
Widor continued to take pupils on a private basis, but only the
most talented were accepted. A considerable number of these
were from the English-speaking world. The blind organist Alfred
Hollins played to him, but the verdict was not very encouraging:
he had 'good mechanism,' but not much more: he had a good
deal to learn'. His subsequent lessons with Guilmant proved
fruitful.[15] J. W. Ibberson of Sheffield spent his summer vacations
from 1897 to 1902 with Widor, who had visited that city to give
recitals on the Cavaillé-Coll organ installed in the Albert Hall in
1873. Ibberson had been appointed Organist-designate of St
Mary's Episcopal Cathedral, Edinburgh, but the death of his
father compelled him to take charge of the family cutlery firm.
For over fifty years he remained organist of Wesley Church,
Fulwood Road, Sheffield, and his friend Vierne dedicated his
Cloches de Hinckley to him.[16]

From Ohio, USA came Albert Riemenschneider for the
summers of 1904 to 1910 to study composition with Widor and
organ with Guilmant. His name is familiar to many students for
his edition of *371 Harmonised Chorales*, part of a comprehensive
edition of the works of J. S. Bach.

A pupil who was to remain particularly close to Widor was
Horace Hawkins. His lessons began in 1913 while organist of St
George's English church in Paris, and continued after the war
during vacations from Hurstpierpoint College where he had
become Director of Music in 1915. From 1938-58 he was
organist of Chichester Cathedral. An outstanding choirmaster
and player in the French style, he continued his master's tradition of liturgical improvisation. As well as being an advocate of
plainchant in the Anglican services, he was at the same time an
active performer of contemporary music, conducting the British
première of Poulenc's Organ Concerto in 1944.[17]

Among all Widor's pupils, Albert Schweitzer from Alsace was
unique. A philosopher and theologian by training, he became a
Pastor in the Lutheran Church. At the same time, his gifts as an
organist were exceptional. He met Widor through his uncle who

had business connections in Paris, and his first lesson took place in 1893. Five years later, he left Strasbourg University to work for his Doctorate on the philosophy of Kant at the Sorbonne in Paris, while taking further lessons from Widor. These were continued in the following years, when Schweitzer made his annual visits to the French capital in the spring. He was now a mature man, and the relationship between them was not simply one of master and pupil. In fact, the influence was mutual: Schweitzer learned much in terms of technique and musical architecture, and Widor's own understanding of Bach's chorale preludes was greatly enhanced by the theologian's thorough knowledge of Lutheran hymnody.

Widor confessed that the more he studied these works, the less he understood them: 'Why these almost excessively abrupt antitheses of feeling? Why does [Bach] add contrapuntal motives to a chorale melody that have often no relation to the mood of the melody?' Schweitzer explained that 'many things in the chorales must seem obscure to you, for the reason that they are only explicable by the texts pertaining to them'. Thus Widor began to realize that Bach's works were not merely models of pure counterpoint but rather manifest 'an unparalleled desire and capacity for expressing poetic ideas and for bringing word and tone into unity'.[18]

Widor suggested that Schweitzer's specialist knowledge of the historical and theological dimensions to Bach's music should be given wider currency. The result was the book *J. S. Bach: le musicien-poète* (1905) which first appeared in French, and later, expanded, in German (1908) and English (1911) editions. Coloured as they were by the aesthetics of Wagner, his ideas played an important part in dispelling the widely-held view of Bach as a dry pedant. Widor helped by writing introductions, as he had previously done for Pirro's *l'Orgue de Jean-Sébastien Bach* (1895) and *Johann Sébastien Bach* (1902). The organist of Saint-Sulpice showed himself both open-minded and courageous in publicly associating himself with a Protestant biblical scholar; for at the time when Schweitzer published his *Von Reimarus zu Wrede* (Quest for the Historical Jesus) (1906)—which claimed that Christ himself believed in the actual future establishment of God's Kingdom on Earth—Alfred Loisy and the Modernist movement were being firmly suppressed by Pius X for attempting to make a synthesis of Catholic theology and biblical criticism.[19]

Meanwhile, Schweitzer had discovered yet another vocation—
to train to become a medical missionary, much to Widor's
horror. He tried to dissuade him, but received the reply: 'Yes,
Maître, but God calls me.' As Hawkins tells us, Widor 'went
around dazed for some time, continually exclaiming "Mon Dieu,
Mon Dieu!"'[20] Nevertheless, the indefatigable Schweitzer found
time to found, together with Widor, the Paris Bach Society in
1905. Its conductor, Gustave Bret, Widor's assistant at Saint-
Sulpice, insisted on Schweitzer as organ continuo player in the
concerts, which he carried out with his usual conscientiousness
and complete self-effacement.[21]

Schweitzer was also organist for the concerts of the church of
Saint-Guillaume in his home town of Strasbourg. Widor and Bret
together made frequent return visits there for these concerts conducted by Ernest Munch, in which the cantatas and passions of
Bach were regularly performed. Sometimes Widor played the solo
part in one of his own works for organ and orchestra. These
occasions made a great impression on Munch's young son
Charles, the future conductor:

I used to attend their rehearsals and afterward listen to these great men
argue bitterly about details of interpretation. Their debate sometimes
took so violent a turn that my mother had to run to the protection of her
furniture. The scarcity of dynamic indications in 17th. and 18th.
century scores occasioned passionate controversy. The opinions of the
most important musicologists were passed in review, the solutions of
other conductors considered, and finally all reasoning was abandoned
and each spoke from his heart alone. It was from this, I believe, that I
really learned to love music.[22]

Widor had a special affection for Schweitzer, admiring 'the
altruism, the high intelligence, the spirit of sacrifice of this pupil
who became his friend'.[23] In his company, a window was opened
into the old sceptic's soul, leading him to declare that 'except for
certain Preludes and Fugues of Bach, I can no longer think of any
organ art as holy which is not consecrated to the church through
its themes, whether it be from the chorale or from the Gregorian
chant'. Once, when they were together at the organ of Notre
Dame 'as the rays of the setting sun streamed through the dusk of
the nave in transfigured peace', he was moved to a rhetorical
utterance not unworthy of Victor Hugo: 'organ playing is the
manifestation of a will filled with the vision of eternity'.[24]

When Widor was elected a Corresponding Member of the Berlin Academy in 1906, Schweitzer made the suggestion that he compose a work for organ and orchestra as an act of thanks. The resulting Sinfonia Sacra, Op. 81 (1908) is based on the chorale 'Come, Saviour of the Heathen', which they chose together.[25] This melody appears in the opening Adagio, and in the Finale, where it is played successively by the organ, trombones, and woodwind as an independent part to the brittle neo-classical fugue in the strings. In the autumn of 1911, Schweitzer played it at the Munich Festival of French Music. On this occasion, Widor, though conducting, had dined too well at the invitation of a champagne magnate, and arrived late for the concert. 'He rushed to the rostrum and began at once to conduct with one hand, while searching for his glasses with the other. His baton changing hands, he searched in his pockets. His glasses were found a quarter of the way through.' Only Schweitzer's firm playing saved the day; he certainly had earned his fee, which paid for his medical examinations.[26]

There seemed no limit to his commitments. In 1911, Widor invited him to collaborate with him on a new edition of Bach's organ works, which G. Schirmer of New York had commissioned from him. Their idea was to produce an *Urtext*—a pure reproduction of what Bach actually wrote down—but with introductions 'showing to organists acquainted with modern organs only, and therefore strangers to the organ style of Bach, what registration and what changes of keyboard had to be considered for any particular piece on the organs with which Bach had to reckon'.

This edition was essentially pragmatic in its aims, allowing for 'a greater variation in volume and gradations of tone than Bach could manage upon his organs . . . but the supreme rule must always be that . . . sufficient prominence be given to the lines of the melody, the effects that may be secured by the tone-colour being treated as of secondary importance'. Schweitzer would prepare rough drafts, and the two then met in Paris or Günsburg to work them out.[27]

Only the first five volumes were completed under their joint efforts, for in 1913, Schweitzer left Europe to found a hospital in Lambarene (Gabon). In March, he embarked at Bordeaux for Africa, his effects including a zinc-lined piano with pedal attachment, presented to him by the Paris Bach Society. He had originally intended to produce further rough drafts in Africa for the three volumes of choral preludes, but more pressing tasks forced him to postpone the project until after Widor's death. That part achieved together was published in French, German, and English (1912-14) but, for financial reasons, was bought mainly in the English-speaking world.[28]

In Germany, Bach was regarded as the epitome of Protestantism, but the emphasis given to him by Widor and Schweitzer as a universal figure helped to integrate his music into the Catholic sphere. This achievement is all the more remarkable in view of the hostility shown by the Catholic establishment towards German culture and ideas—such as science, biblical criticism, or Wagner's operas—which Liberals and freethinkers encouraged. Today, it is quite accepted that Bach can stand beside Palestrina in the Catholic liturgy, for, in Widor's own words. 'Bach is on the whole the most universal of artists. What speaks through his works is pure religious emotion; and this is one and the same in all men, in spite of the national and religious partitions in which we are born and bred.'[29]

THE CULTURAL AMBASSADOR

THE Institut de France, which occupies an impressive seventeenth-century building on the Quai d'Orsay, purports to be the guardian of the highest scientific, intellectual, and artistic traditions of the nation. Founded in 1795, it is divided into five Académies: of these, the Académie des Beaux-Arts (formerly the Académie Royale de Peinture et Sculpture, founded in 1648) is reserved for composers, painters, sculptors, architects, and engravers. Its membership included Cherubini, Halévy, and Berlioz.

At the Institut, Widor joined Fauré, Dubois, Massenet, Saint-Saëns, Bourget, Coppée, Carolus Duran, Bonnat, Hanotaux, and Lamy, as well as being introduced to a new circle which included Henri Bergson, philosopher of the *élan vital*, Maurice Barrès, author of the *culte du moi*, and General Lyautey, who built up the Protectorate of Morocco.

It seemed to some that Widor had at last given way to the French cultural bureaucracy. Ferruccio Busoni, whom Philipp was anxious to bring to Paris, was visiting the city in 1912 with the vague idea of buying a house. The great pianist was amused at a comment of Widor, who appeared to betray the mentality of *la France fonctionnaire*: 'When you acquire a property, you will be counted as one of our own people.' Busoni, however, soon perceived the essence of the man; and in subsequent visits never failed to get together with Widor and Philipp at Foyot's, when he would keep them informed about the latest artistic trends and his own musical philosophy.[1]

1914 was to be a momentous year for Widor. At the age of 70, and with no previous administrative experience, he was chosen by his fellow members to be Permanent Secretary of the Académie des Beaux-Arts. It proved to be an inspired appointment in every way, for, in addition to his musical qualifications, his outstanding knowledge of the visual arts earned him the respect of their practi-

tioners, as Pierné admitted: 'Let an engraver, or a painter, or a
sculptor ask for some information or make a slip, Widor will
answer or correct the error. What a mine of information!'[2] Saint-
Saëns rose to the occasion with a welcoming poem:

> Grand musicien, cher confrère,
> Doux et lumineux secrétaire
> Toi dont la perpétuité
> Nous remplit de joyeuseté
> Puisse Minerve la guerrière
> Patronne de notre maison
> Protéger ta belle carrière,
> Etendre son bras sur ton front![3]

The euphoria, however, was to be short lived. Within a month,
the Great War had begun. This event was an unmitigated disaster
for the civilized values which Widor believed in. The parallel with
1870, when he took up his post at Saint-Sulpice, was all too
apparent. In retrospect, even he doubted that he would have
accepted the secretaryship, had the circumstances been
foreseeable with all the additional burdens entailed. On
31 August he and Bonnat were urgently summoned to the
Louvre to supervise the removal of 766 of the finest art treasures
to a safer location at Toulouse.

Both men were deeply affected by the melancholy sight of the
rolled-up canvasses and sculptures torn from the peace of their
temple and unceremoniously packed into crates for their journey
in six padded wagons. The galleries, their walls denuded of paintings, and the floors littered with planks, straw, and tools, evoked
disturbing memories of the Franco-Prussian War.[4] Paris itself was
blacked out in fear of attack from the air. In Widor's own description, the city was now 'a sepulchre; no longer any lights . . . un-
forgettable the crossing of the Seine: water without movement or
reflection surrounded by sombre piles, indefinite in outline. A
deathly silence. It was terrible, but magnificent.'[5]

With the rapid advance of the German armies, Paris became
threatened. On 1 September the Government left for Bordeaux.
Much discussion ensued between it and the Institut as to the
position of the Presidents and Permanent Secretaries of the
Académies who were responsible for the funds of their institutions. It was feared that, in the event of the fall of the capital, they
might be held to ransom. At first, it was thought expedient that

they follow the Government if the order were given, despite protests that such a course was not in the traditions of the Institut. On 3 September the Conseil de Ministres decided to leave them free to make their own individual decisions.[6]

Widor and some of his colleagues had adopted a restaurant in the rue Royale which was frequented by the General Staff of the Allied armies, Italian and British war correspondents, airmen, and drivers of Generals; it was a veritable centre of information. On 5 September he was privy to the top-secret admission that

the camp cut off at Paris can hardly resist more than three or four days: it would be enough to put one of our forts out of action for the enemy to enter by the breach and force our gates. On Thursday or Friday, General Galieni will be killed at the head of his troops; *he will have fulfilled his commission right to the end*. This was to be the final act: taken by storm, Paris would be plundered, sacked and burned . . . with this mournful vision of our country before us, we parted without a word.[7]

During that terrible week,

we heard the guns, we knew nothing. We were only astonished, without drawing any conclusions, that the gunfire seemed gradually to grow more distant. On September 11, Elie Berger arrived from Chantilly, where he was keeper of the castle. He informed us that Chantilly had been occupied for 24 hours: then suddenly, the German forces were evacuated. That was all he knew. The following day, we learned about the victory of the Marne.[8]

The Russians had mobilized with unexpected rapidity, and, to counter their attack in the East, the Germans withdrew two army corps from France.

Returning to his desk at the Institut, Widor confronted the problems of wartime with all his superabundant energy, always keeping an even temper and complete self-control. It was entirely characteristic of him that he did not use his position for his own self-aggrandizement; on the contrary, he only wore his decorations of an Officer of the Legion of Honour at the annual meeting of the Académie.[9] For most men, the normal day-to-day running of the establishment—involving endless meetings of the Commission Administrative Centrale, financial matters, and library provisions—would, in such trying conditions, have been a sufficient task. But in addition, Widor took it upon himself in his official capacity to help artists and musicians in need: Philipp, the

President of the Association of Former Pupils of the Conservatoire, described himself as 'an official beggar'.[10] It was Widor's
influence which resulted in Schweitzer's hospital in Lambarene
being reopened: as he was a German citizen, it had been closed
down at the outbreak of the war.[11]

Widor also showed his mettle in the matter of electing new
members. Many men would have been content to preserve the
Institut as a kind of old boys' club, but he was concerned rather
with its self-renewal: that it should represent the best artistic
achievement of the time, for the danger always existed that its
traditional conservation of the eternal principles of art was liable
to degenerate into obscurantism. He therefore invited Debussy
and the sculptor Rodin to present themselves as candidates, even
though, according to Philipp, neither of them liked him. His plan,
however, ended in disappointment.[12]

Debussy's election was delayed until 1918, due to the machi-
nations of Saint-Saëns who wrote to Fauré: 'I advise you to look at
the pieces for two pianos, *Noir et Blanc* which M. Debussy has just
published. It is unbelievable, and we must at all costs bar the door of
the Institut to a gentleman capable of such atrocities, fit to be placed
beside cubist paintings.'[13] The matter was finally resolved by
Debussy's death before the election took place.

The previous year (1917), Rodin's candidature had been greeted
with violent protests in certain artistic quarters. A petition was
launched, but Widor managed to snuff it out at the point when the
members of the Institut were being solicited. This incident actually
strengthened Rodin's position, for 27 Academicians came out in
open support of him. But, for the second time, Widor's hopes were
dashed: 'On the Saturday, 24 November, the day fixed for the
election, I had the sad honour to stand before Rodin's coffin and
announce his success.'[14]

Undoubtedly, Widor's greatest endeavours were in the field of
international cultural relations. At the height of the war and even at
the moments of greatest national danger, he foresaw the need also to
win the subsequent peace. He became a prime mover in forging
firmer links with the English-speaking peoples in particular, in
recognition of the military alliance which saved France from
ultimate defeat.

As it happened, a small domestic incident had unforeseen con-
sequences. In 1915, Widor moved into rooms in the Institut. He

was permitted to house his chamber organ in the Musée de Caen, which he converted from a lumber-room into a delightful concert-hall and gallery. From the outset, it was made to serve the war effort. He was shocked that no effort was being made to recognize the devoted services of the American nurses tending the wounded in France. In October 1916, he organized a small concert in their honour, during which Bergson delivered a vote of thanks in English. The guests were deeply moved by this sincere gesture.

After the war, the idea of a monthly series of concerts was adopted, to foster international goodwill and serve as a focal point for friends from other countries, national representatives, ambassadors, and ministers. 'Three-quarters of an hour of music and a cup of tea,' as Widor worded the invitation cards. The management of the concerts was entrusted to Philipp. Saint-Saëns took part on two occasions, and rarely performed chamber works by Glazounov, Dvořák, and Busoni were given an opportunity to be heard. [15]

It was Spain which next claimed Widor's attention, notwithstanding its state of neutrality and the hostility of its upper classes towards France and the United States. In April 1916, Widor, Lamy, and Bergson were members of a fact-finding mission sent to Madrid by the Minister for Foreign Affairs to discover Spanish opinion of France, to study its institutions, and greet its leaders in the arts, sciences, and politics. An entire week was reserved at the Ateneo, a free university, where an enthusiastic audience of 500 gathered to listen to lectures by the various Frenchmen. Bergson sent a thrill through the hall with his description of the spirit of the women of France in those tragic hours. To succeed such an accomplished speaker was a daunting task for Widor on the following day. He presented a characteristically wide-ranging survey of musical history, while Bergson sat in front of him, giving moral support.

However, Widor did not feel it was going well. Towards the end, he broke off abruptly with the following coda:

Your country is a veritable home of the arts, of monuments without equal, of masterpieces of painting, one of the most beautiful museums of the world. Among you, Bonnat, Henri Regnault, Carolus Duran and many others have felt their hearts beat and have been strengthened in their calling. How can it be that when our students at the Villa Medici have completed their time in Rome, they return directly to Paris without going to contemplate and study Velasquez? [16]

Widor could hardly have foreseen the result of his spontaneous tribute to his hosts. A castle in Spain was—literally—to rise. The French party were invited to a reception by the ill-fated King Alphonso XIII, forced into exile fifteen years later. It was Winston Churchill who remarked on the king's deep regard for England and his admission that 'only I and the mob are for the Allies'.[17] But the strength and prestige of Spain was his over-riding concern, for he was conscious that his country was a European cul-de-sac. He made a proposition to Widor that if the French were prepared to raise money to build a cultural centre to attract their students to Spain, he would find the land on which to build it. The Académie gratefully accepted this offer, and in 1919, it was duly ceded a parcel of land by decree of the Cortes, after long negotiations.[18]

In the interim, Alphonso had asked Widor to organize an exhibition of contemporary French painting, which was held in the Palais du Retiro, Madrid in May 1918 with great success. Before being transported to Spain, the paintings were stored in the Musée de Caen at the time when long-range shells from the 'Big Berthas' were falling dangerously close, and Widor hardly slept.[19] Indeed, splinters from a bomb which fell on the Pont des Arts were showered on his table; he himself stuck pieces of paper over the broken window panes.[20]

The Casa Velasquez was planned to rise on the plateau of the Moncloa where it was believed that the Spanish master once had a country house. A magnificent view extended to the Sierra de Guadarrama. On 22 May 1920 Alphonso presided over a brilliant ceremony to mark the laying of the foundation stone; he was surrounded by two Queens—his wife Victoria and his mother, Marie-Christine—, his ministers, bishops, and clergy, and a brigade of infantry. Distinguished representatives of France were also present, including Widor himself. The Municipality of Madrid made a valuable donation of a monumental portico, preserved from the recently demolished Palais d'Oñate. Comprising two storeys and balconies, its numbered stones were reconstructed to form the facade of the Casa Velasquez. 'We should salute chivalrous Spain at the threshold of the house of France', exclaimed Widor.[21]

Meanwhile, funds were required to complete the building. The Baron Edmond de Rothschild—a member of the Paris branch of the great banking family and an expert on engravings—was approached by Widor. He agreed to contribute to a limited extent, for his true interest lay in London. The times indicated that a cultural liaison between Britain and France was a matter of greater urgency, for all the romanticism of the Madrid venture.

Thus Rothschild promised to give his full support to the establishment of a cultural centre in London. A search for suitable premises was at once got under way, and Widor and Rothschild visited London together in May 1919 to inspect Grosby Hall in Chelsea, the remains of the fifteenth-century palace of Sir Thomas More. Although its historical associations appealed to Widor, the building—swarming with Belgian refugees—was deemed uninhabitable.

At this point Sir John Simpson, a Corresponding Member of the Institut and President of the Royal Society of Architects, took a hand, offering to relieve the Frenchmen of their search. A few days later, Simpson telegraphed Paris that he had discovered a suitable property. Widor and Rothschild immediately set out again for London. Widor described the exciting Channel crossing:

At Boulogne, ships and transports loaded with English troops crowded picturesquely on the deck, returning to their own country. *Rule Britannia* answers *God save the King*. We sail surrounded by a veritable fleet. At Dover, we are held up by the disembarcation of brigades returning from the Rhine, thousands of men. As soon as they set foot on the jetty, they form columns and mark time. In London, French troops are camping in Hyde Park. Foch is at Buckingham Palace.

On their arrival in London, Simpson took them to inspect a spacious house at the corner of Queen's Gate and Prince Consort Road, facing the Albert Hall. A garden separated it from the Royal College of Music. A central hall opened onto a library and a dining room, and the two upper storeys contained twenty rooms. They were pleasantly surprised to find the house decorated with engravings and French reproductions, for it had been built by an art-lover, a M. Vivian, nearly fifty years earlier.

After a detailed inspection, it was pronounced the very house dreamed of. Rothschild purchased it immediately without any financial negotiations and presented it as a gift to the Institut, to 'promote the development of intellectual relations between France and England'. On the following day, Widor watched the

Victory Parade from the balcony of Lady de Rothschild's house in Piccadilly. Five days before, he had been present at the Parade in Paris, and again he thrilled to the sight of the march-past and the crowds cheering the heroes of the war.[22]

This eventful year also included the London performance of the Sinfonia Sacra at the Henry Wood Promenade Concerts on 18 September. For the *Musical Times*, this was a 'not very attractive work . . . not Widor at his best', although the organ soloist Stanley Marchant 'played brilliantly'.[23] These British connections were further cemented in March 1920, when Edward Elgar was elected a Corresponding Member of the Académie des Beaux-Arts, an honour which gave enormous pleasure to his wife before her death one month later. His note of admission, signed by Widor, was placed in her coffin before burial.[24]

The official opening of the Maison à Londres—originally planned to coincide with the visit of the French President, Raymond Poincaré, to Britain—was postponed, as the work of adapting the building to its new purpose had not been completed on schedule. A hurried, perfunctory ceremony took place the following year on a foggy winter day. However, on 26 February 1921, a distinguished delegation of scientists and artists were present in London for the opening of the French Lycée. This was Widor's opportunity to invite them to visit the Maison, and they were duly overwhelmed by the magnificent opportunities which it offered. The French Ambassador jestingly offered to exchange buildings with the Director of the Maison! To bring this spontaneous occasion to its close, Widor played 'God save the King' and the 'Marseillaise' on the piano.[25]

Amid this whirlwind campaign, Widor found time to make a conquest of a very different nature. Having already made his entry into the respectable worlds of the Conservatoire and the Institut, matrimony was the remaining institution which beckoned to him. This was indeed an extraordinary step for a man of 76 to take. He had always been very susceptible to female charms and had not denied himself the pleasures of the flesh. In old age, however, a regular union doubtlessly appealed to him as a bulwark against the fear of loneliness and approaching death.

On 26 April 1920, at Charchigné, Mayenne, he was married to Mathilde de Montesquiou-Fezeusac.[26] Very much younger than her husband, she was the niece of the Anglophile Mme Hélène Standish—descended from the aristocratic Decazes family—who reputedly looked like Queen Alexandra and even dressed like her. [27] Mathilde had originally set her cap at Marcel Proust, but failing him, her second choice was Widor! Leaving his quarters at the Institut, he moved into his new married home at 3 rue Belloy. As it happened, Proust was living in the adjacent rue Hamelin (No. 44), and could look into the Widors' dining room. He was fascinated by the pre-war grandeur of their lifestyle, the meals served with china and candlesticks, and the relationships between the Widors and Mme Standish. [28]

Ever on the move, Widor played a leading part in the setting up of the Franco-American Conservatoire at Fontainebleau, a venture which grew out of the requirements of the US Forces in France. To solve the acute shortage of bandsmen, General Pershing turned to Walter Damrosch, conductor of the New York Philharmonic Orchestra, for help. The result took the form of a travelling Conservatoire, which enlisted the services of French instrumental teachers. Professional pianists and violinists were rapidly converted into clarinettists and cornet players. From time to time, many of these sought permission to travel to Paris to take lessons on their main instruments from the leading Professors.

After the war and the return of the US Army, a strong desire was expressed that these musical links should continue. Requests for lessons in the summer vacations were made, which led to the establishment of a special summer school for Americans, with Widor as the first Director-General (1921-3). This was held in the Louis XV wing of the Palais de Fontainebleau. The opening took place on 26 June 1921, presided over by Widor, Damrosch and the Minister of Public Instruction, Léon Bérard. [29] Damrosch exhorted the students to 'learn French and the French people . . . their civilisation must be kept for the benefit of the world . . .'. [30]

The Professors included Philipp, Paul Vidal, and Widor himself. But it was the much younger Nadia Boulanger who made the greatest impact and influenced an entire generation of American composers. Aaron Copland was one of many who stayed on in France to study composition with her. He had been somewhat put out by Widor, who introduced him at one of the student concerts as 'a young American composer of modern tendencies'. To Copland, on the other hand, Widor seemed to be merely an 'ancient organist and composer'.[31] But this was unfair to the old man who was throwing himself into the school, giving recitals, and doing his utmost to make the students welcome: before leaving his classes, he would shake each student's hand at least five times![32]

Meanwhile, work on the Casa Velasquez had run into problems. The architect died suddenly and was replaced by the architect of the Louvre, Camille Lefèvre. Funds at first were forthcoming from Rothschild; Bérard promised the support of the government; and General Lyautey—a man of vast culture who enticed poets and musicians to perform in his desert camps—contributed 40,000 francs on behalf of the Cherif and Moroccan Protectorate. But suddenly catastrophe struck. On 15 January 1922 Briand's government fell, and Poincaré succeeded him as President. A lawyer of unimpeachable honesty, he saw his primary task to be the reduction of government expenditure and inflation, opposing the idea of state subsidies.

It was fully apparent that if the new government were to refuse to honour the financial commitment of its predecessor, the entire Casa Velasquez project would fall to the ground: an acutely embarrassing situation both with regard to Spain and to those who had already made generous donations. It fell to Widor to tackle Poincaré directly one evening at the Dutch Embassy; the former recorded the following conversation: 'M. le Président, we need your help urgently, some official support!—You must not hope for, or expect anything, for the Chambers will do nothing.—But we are committed, it is a question of honour, you are condemning me to suicide!—I have already seen Gounod die.—Gounod did not commit suicide!—You have the Villa Medici and . . . the Maison de Londres, what more do you want?—We have Rome and London indeed, but we still need Madrid . . . for our intellectual expansion . . . which works unremittingly for the peace of the world. *Pax hominibus bonae voluntatis.*'

This lofty vision—which also inspired Bergson as President of the 'Commission Internationale de Coopération Intellectuelle', set up by the League of Nations[33]—ultimately could not fail to move Poincaré, himself a lover of literature and a member of the Institut. He proceeded to study the matter in person and put it before the *Chambre des députés*, which voted a grant of

.3,500,000 francs. A committee of 'The Friends of the Casa Velasquez' was formed with Lyautey as President,[34] and King Alphonso expressed his gratitude to Widor in a personal visit to his home in Paris.[35]

10

AN INDIAN SUMMER

THE years following the Great War witnessed the sharp decline of Widor's world. The qualities of elegance and decorum, the Romantic spirit tempered by a Classical sense of order, now seemed to be swept aside in an age which was experiencing the speeding up of historical change in the aftermath of the violence unleashed by world conflict. The arts were employing shock tactics against established forms and conventions. The *Mona Lisa* was reproduced with added moustache; Marcel Duchamps had held an exhibition in a public lavatory. The deliberate destructiveness of the Dada movement was absorbed into Surrealism with its cult of dreams and the unconscious mind, inspired by Freud's theories.

Widor's former pupils, Milhaud and Honegger, were now leading members of the group *Les Six*, which was having its own milder and less radical protest in the form of flirtations with jazz, Latin-American and music-hall cultures, and pastiches of classical styles. This 'Cocteau aesthetic' did not meet with Widor's approval. On learning that Milhaud's Brazilian-inspired ballet score *Le Bœuf sur le toit* was to be the French contribution to the 1922 Salzburg Festival, he exploded:

What a tasteless joke from *les copains*. The programme . . . bears exclusively the names of the blasphemers, and is unaware of Mozart. I wouldn't be happy that money obtained from the Maison de la Musique be used to subsidize this delegation of 'French' Bolsheviks, which ought to be sent to Lenin rather than Salzburg, to get a foretaste of punishments which surely await it in a better world.[1]

In this atmosphere of revolt, old established institutions came under fire. A student rhyme went:

> Je hais les tours de Saint-Sulpice:
> Quand par hazard je les rencontre,
> Je pisse
> Contre.[2]

Ravel refused the Legion of Honour in January 1920. The Institut was all too readily misunderstood and taken as a symbol of gerontocracy, the domination of the hated Generals and politicians who had sacrificed a generation in war. Unhappily, Widor's final opera *Nerto* also appeared an anachronism at its première at the Paris Opéra in October 1924, having had to wait thirty years for this occasion. Its libretto by Maurice Lena (based on a play by Mistral) re-enacts the medieval story of a maiden whose soul is sold to the Devil by her dissolute father. This lyric drama drew Dumesnil's criticism that 'it was hardly surprising that it had aged after such a long period'.[3]

Despite these disturbances in the outside world, Widor continued to devote himself to the Académie des Beaux-Arts. He even found himself drawn to Dubois, and they frequently discussed the problems of housing the musical archives for which they were responsible. The question arose as to whether they should remain dispersed or brought together. The latter proposal filled Widor with alarm: 'But would that not be rash? Is it wise to gather so many masterpieces in one place? Is it not a great sadness that there must be that logical certainty that there is no building which fire or war cannot destroy? Every morning from my window I contemplate the ordered magnificence of the Louvre, and every day I tremble for the Louvre.' Widor's counsel prevailed, and the priceless collections remained at the Conservatoire, the Mazarine Library, the Bibliothèque Nationale, Sainte-Geneviève, and the Opéra.[4]

Widor's nucleus of friends remained faithful. Philipp remained a constant companion, both at the Conservatoire and at the Café de Paris, for which he had forsaken Foyot's, 33 rue de Tournon, demolished to make way for the Place Francis Poulenc. Widor's house at 3 rue Belloy has also been sacrificed to developers, alas.[5] Schweitzer never failed to visit him on his returns to Europe in 1927, 1932, and 1934: he would listen to his old master improvising at Saint-Sulpice 'with head in hands, lost in contemplation'.[6] Hawkins—for whom Mme Widor had a particular liking—maintained regular contact during holidays from Hurstpierpoint College. His wife died tragically in 1927, leaving a surviving daughter, Ann: Widor agreed to become her godfather. His duties, however, did not extend much beyond presenting the infant with a signed photograph of himself! Her other godparents were Siegfried and Winifred Wagner, also friends of this singularly well-connected schoolmaster.[7]

Vierne and Dupré, however, had complicated matters by a serious quarrel between themselves. Dupré, who had stood in as acting organist of Notre Dame during Vierne's convalescence in Switzerland, made a recital tour of America billed as 'Organist of Notre Dame'. Although it is highly unlikely that Dupré himself was responsible, Vierne—a sick man who had lost his sense of proportion—was mortally offended.[8]

In December 1925, Gigout died, and the Organ Professorship at the Conservatoire at last reverted to Widor's own line of succession. The main candidates were Dupré, Tournemire, Libert, and Vierne: the last-named withdrew at the final moment. Tournemire had been Professor of Chamber Music since 1919, but it was Dupré who was successful.[9] He proved a most distinguished teacher, not allowing his brilliant international career as a recitalist to interfere with his new duties. Widor, however, could still exert his authority. In the early 1930s, André Marchal—Gigout's pupil—was invited to play for a wedding at Saint-Sulpice. During his performance of Bach's Prelude and Fugue in G major, BWV 541, he felt Widor's hand pumping his shoulder to indicate a slower tempo![10]

Despite advancing years, Widor continued to take his composition class at the Conservatoire. His students found him in truth a man who (in Kipling's words) could 'walk with Kings—nor lose the common touch', always very warm in his relations with them. By this time, however, he was content to coast along, frequently arriving late after gossiping with Philipp in the adjoining class,[11] engaging the students in conversation, or singling out Yvonne Lefébure to play the piano. The disciplines of fugue were devolved upon his assistant, Ganay. After Mlle Lefébure had won her First Prize for fugue, she visited Widor to show him her written work—for the first time! After a brief word of congratulation, he steered her to the piano, requesting a performance of the 'Appassionata'. While she played, he improvised added chords which fitted Beethoven's text perfectly![12]

Widor finally retired from his Professorship in October 1927, handing over the class to Paul Dukas, 'whose noble character and fine talent', Philipp tells us, 'he admired'. Dukas took on the responsibility for a new and highly gifted generation, which included Olivier Messiaen, Jean Langlais, and Maurice Duruflé. Unfortunately, the Institut seems to have been a psychological barrier to any contact between them and Widor. Messiaen was too shy to approach him there; moreover, his two attempts at the Prix de Rome in 1929 and 1930 were unsuccessful. [13]

With the revival of interest in mysticism between the wars, it was Tournemire who attracted this élite group to Sainte-Clotilde to experience his transcendental improvisations. His compositional masterpiece, the *l'Orgue Mystique* (1927-32), based on Gregorian chant, is the Roman Catholic reply to Bach's cantatas, and consists of suites of movements for the Mass for every Sunday of the church's year. In this work, the spirit of the thirteenth century and its Gothic cathedrals is vividly recreated.

It was a nice coincidence that the year 1927—which saw the start of Tournemire's great project—also marked Widor's return to organ composition after two decades. His *Suite Latine*, Op. 86 is likewise based on Gregorian themes in three of its six movements. While this late flowering of his art breaks no new ground, remaining stylistically self-sufficient and immune to fashion, a further renewal of the religious spirit is in evidence. Widor may well have been stimulated by his colleagues at the Institut, Bergson and the Abbé Henri Bremond, who were working on their respective books *Deux sources de la morale et de la religion* and *Histoire littéraire du sentiment religieux en France*.

The grave beauty of the 'Praeludium', 'Lamento', and Adagio of the *Suite Latine* is achieved by a successful integration of expressive chromatic lines into a clear tonal scheme without strain or harshness. But most striking are the Gregorian movements. The 'Beatus Vir' radiates a simple charm with its easy flow of diatonic melody, yet a subtle rhythmic dimension is provided by the division of the basic crotchet pulse into changing groups of three and two quavers. Particularly bold in conception is the 'Ave Maris Stella'. Far from the comforting sentimentality of conventional Mariolatry, this star burns fiercely in extended passages of trills and bare open fifth sonorities. Finally, the 'Lauda Sion' combines the brilliance of a toccata with the heavy tread of a march.

Writing books also absorbed his energy. In 1923, he had brought out his little *Initiation musicale*, which filled an important gap in French education, namely its under-development of popular musical appreciation. He revels in the broad sweeps of musical history from ancient times, yet expressing himself with great concision. Technical aspects are lucidly covered, with due emphasis on acoustics.

Four years later, there appeared his *Académie des Beaux-Arts: fondations et portraits*. One of Widor's duties was to write notices to mark the deaths of fellow Académiciens. His generation were now coming to the end of their lives, leaving him as the last survivor. Amongst others, Massenet had died in 1912, Carolus Duran in 1916, Saint-Saëns in 1921, and Fauré and Dubois in 1924. Widor's task was to continue the tradition of the *Eloges*, monumental commemorations of the virtues of the dead, with criticism suppressed. He struck exactly the right tone, avoiding the pitfalls of pomposity and morbid rhetoric, preserving his usual style, terse yet buoyant, and enlivened with humorous anecdotes, all in perfect taste.

It was certainly not the occasion to settle old scores, but to give each man his due. No longer 'the man of consecutive octaves', Dubois was accorded 'the honour of having codified the principles of our art. A great educator, man of the rule and discipline, he had a fear of hurting his pupils by too direct criticism'. Saint-Saëns was extolled as 'the greatest French symphonist . . . He was generous, but of an anonymous generosity.' These notices are a mine of information concerning the affairs of the Institut. But it is surely significant that Widor omitted Fauré's notice in his published collection.

For all that he had become a pillar of French civilization he did not forget his eastern European origins: in 1926, the Insignias of the Order *Polonia Restituta* were presented to him. Four years later, the White Russian General, Paul de Maximovich—formerly Chief of Staff of the Russian Cavalry, but now an émigré in France—sent him a photograph of five German flags captured from Hindenburg's army in 1914. This gift was in recognition of the musical help given to his family: his wife had been sent to Widor by Safonoff, and now his daughter Marie was being given the honour of taking part in a concert of Widor's works under the composer's baton.[14]

Meanwhile Widor continued to enhance the dignity and grandeur of the services at Saint-Sulpice. Among the worshippers in the early 1920s was the future Existentialist philosopher,

Simone de Beauvoir, then passing through an adolescent religious crisis.[15] Felix Aprahamian, the English critic, recalls a visit to the church in 1933. As he entered the 'Petit Orgue' was playing. But as he was about to go up to the 'Grand Orgue', he was suddenly transfixed by a blinding full organ chord of C major: Widor had arrived. The old man of 89 invited the youth of 19 to sit beside him while he played a movement from the *Suite Latine*. Aprahamian observed that for Widor, the marking < > indicated the opening of the swell box, not the addition of stops—so different from the practice of British organists at that time.[16]

On 19 January 1930 a magnificent service was held to celebrate the sixtieth anniversary of his début at Saint-Sulpice. The occasion was dignified by the presence of the Archbishop of Paris, Cardinal Verdier, and the music included Widor's own resplendent setting of the Mass.[17] The following year, he visited Rouen for the Anniversary of the death of Joan of Arc in the company of the Archbishop of Westminster, Cardinal Bourne, a former Sulpician.[18]

In July of that year, Hawkins received an invitation to bring the choir of Hurstpierpoint College to give a concert in the Musée de Caen. It had the distinction of being the first school choir to be broadcast by the BBC. En route for Paris, a final practice was held on the train in preparation for the concert on the following day. It was a glittering social occasion: the distinguished audience included the Senator of Rome, Marcel Dupré, Mme Standish, and the choirmasters from the leading churches of Paris. The boys sang the *Laudate nomen Domini* by the sixteenth-century English composer, Christopher Tye, and Widor's own *Ave Verum Corpus*, specially composed for Hawkins. Widor played two movements of his *Suite Latine* on the organ. After the concert, the choir were 'entertained to the best refreshments that Paris could provide'. Before returning to England, they revisited the Institut to be photographed with Widor. Their final cheers of 'Vive la France!' were gamely answered by the grand old man with 'Vive l'Angleterre!'[19]

1932 was an exceptionally busy year for a man of Widor's age. In March, he gave the opening recital at the Salzburg Festival with the Symphonie 'Gothique' and the *Suite Latine*. A month later, he was making a gramophone recording on the organ at Saint-Sulpice. Indeed, this was not his initiation into the modern world of technology, for he had already, three years before, recorded two movements from *La Korrigane* for Pathé. (In a few precious moments at the end, his voice is heard indistinctly.) For the 1932 recording, produced by Piero Coppola, Widor chose the 'Toccata' from his Symphonie No. 5, and the first two movements and the concluding section of the Finale of the Symphonie 'Gothique'. After some problems with the microphone placing and the acoustics of the church, the session began at 9.00 in the evening and lasted until midnight; then Widor—who showed no sign of fatigue—took Coppola for a stroll in the rain without an umbrella. 'He scoffed at all the Swedish gymnastics, violent sports and other hygenic inventions', recalled Coppola: 'To live well and long, it is enough to work hard, to eat and drink well, and not to turn your head at a pretty face . . .'. [20]

A formal reunion with an old pupil took place on 10 June when Widor shared the opening recital on the newly rebuilt organ of Notre Dame with Vierne. 64 years earlier Widor had helped to inaugurate it: now he returned to play the Symphonie 'Gothique' to general acclaim. Vierne remarked that 'those who were in the organ loft were amazed seeing Widor coming to grips with an instrument which he hardly knew, and playing faultlessly'. After playing his own *Cathédrales*, the Adagio from the Symphonie No. 3, and *Carillon de Westminster*, Vierne concluded the recital with his master's classic Toccata. [21]

The end, however, was in sight. In 1933, Dupré returned from a recital tour of the United States to find Widor very changed and tired: 'I was waiting for you to come back. You are going to stand in for me at Saint-Sulpice on Sunday, and I want to see you succeed me in my post in my lifetime. In your absence, I have lost my strength in my arms, hands and legs. Consequently I have lost my technique.' [22] The loyal Dupré tried in vain to dissuade him from formally resigning on the last Sunday of 1933, but he remained unshakeable in his resolve, accepting the situation with great serenity. To mark his 64 years of devoted service, he was created Honorary Organist by Cardinal Verdier. The Parish added two extra pedal stops to the organ which Widor had always desired. Throughout 1934 he continued to come to Saint-Sulpice. No longer able to climb the steps to the organ loft, he would listen to Dupré, confirmed as his successor, from the nave. [23]

ly apparent that Widor's mental powers were as
In 1934, he composed his last organ work, the
pièces, Op. 87. Their curious titles emphasize
ood of nostalgia, as if he was bidding farewell to the
... its pleasures: plainchant and the religious dimension is
now significantly absent. 'Classique d'hier' conveys a sense of
faded grandeur. The salon is evoked in 'Mystique' by a gently
sensuous melodic line and pianistic textures, all tinged with
melancholy. Finally comes 'Classique d'aujourd'hui', a shadow
of a toccata, its D minor tonality eschewing the usual brilliance.

For the time being, he was still able to fulfil his functions at the
Académie des Beaux-Arts. On the election of Dukas, he wrote to
the new member:

You don't mind being reminded of my regrets on the subject of your
'anti-academic phobia': it's useless to tell you how happy we are about
your cure in one hour . . . don't worry about protocol. There is only one
tradition to respect—a black suit and white tie. I will come for you in the
library to have the honour and joy of presenting you. [24]

Dukas, greatly touched by the friendliness of his reception, told
Philipp that Widor was 'the most delightful of men, and I could
only admire his prodigious culture'. [25]

Widor's health was further undermined by his obsessive urge
to conduct a performance of his Symphonie No. 3 at Saint-Sulpice
with the Orchestra of the Société des Concerts du Conservatoire
and Dupré at the organ. This concert on 19 April 1934—in aid
of Widor's long-cherished project to rebuild the organ of Saint-
Louis des Invalides—was described by Philipp as 'a real
catastrophe. He no longer had the strength to lift his arm, but
with a desperate effort he insisted upon going on to the end.' [26]

A paralysis of his right arm put Widor under doctor's orders,
and a rest at Chantilly was prescribed. [27] Schweitzer, back again
from Africa, remarked upon both his physical condition and his
unabated appetite for life in a letter to Donald Tovey, Professor of
Music at Edinburgh, who had made a new edition of Bach's *Art
of Fugue* (1931, dedicated to Schweitzer): 'Widor was delighted
with the *Art of Fugue* . . . His right arm is giving him much
trouble. I had a great deal to tell him about you.' [28] But to the eye
of a doctor with experience of rare diseases, a more profound
diagnosis presented itself. Schweitzer confided to Dupré that
Widor was suffering from 'a very slow blood poisoning; the

tissues no longer have the strength to renew themselves. I think that he could still live for about two years.' This opinion proved to be absolutely correct.[29]

In May 1935, the Casa Velasquez—after many vicissitudes— was finally opened in its entirety under the Presidency of Alcala Zamora; King Alphonso, alas, had gone into exile four years earlier. But nothing could have prevented Widor from being there in person

with his faithful doctor Lereboullet and his delightful wife, who by their attentions prolonged his life to its extreme limits. In the hall of the Grand Hotel in Madrid, he welcomed the Duc d'Albe and M. Quinones de Leon, who had been associated with the project from the start, with such a smile: these two faithfuls of Alphonso XIII were allowed to return for the ceremony in an atmosphere of political calm. Yet storm clouds were looming.[30]

Civil war was to break out the following year.

This was Widor's last major public appearance, for during the final 18 months of his life he was confined to his house. He worked right up to the end, revising his Symphonie Antique, and making Dupré correct the proofs for publication.[31] He 'followed the work of the Institut with the closest attention', as Philipp noted, 'and believed that he would be able to return to his desk there!'[32] In this connection, he received a visit from Igor Stravinsky in January 1936, canvassing support for election to the Institut. But in the event, it was Florent Schmitt who was successful.[33]

A final pleasure remained. In July 1936 Hawkins brought his boys to Widor's house to sing to him during the course of another visit to Paris. They performed a short programme of English and French songs, and his own *Ave Maria* 'which pleased him greatly'. Pathetically, he told them that it was the first concert he had heard since he was taken ill, as he was now only allowed to sit in his armchair for a little while each afternoon.[34] But for all his acute suffering, he had not become at all self-absorbed. The Spanish Civil War obsessed his thoughts. His beloved Casa Velasquez was bombarded and left in ruins. Yet his perennial optimism was never extinguished: 'If the Casa is in ruins, we will rebuild it.'[35]

As his life drained away, Widor asked Dupré to 'try to see me every day. In a month I feel it will be all over. I have had enough suffering day and night, but I cannot complain for I have had a beautiful life.'[36] He died on Friday 12 March 1937 at 8 o'clock in the evening. He had left instructions which testify to the essential humility of the man. Declining a State Funeral, he wished only for a simple plainchant Requiem Mass at Saint-Sulpice.[37] On the day before these obsequies, the coffin was taken to the church, and in the evening darkness, friends and relatives gathered in the deserted nave, while Dupré played music by Bach.[38]

The following day the French establishment turned out in force to pay their respects, for, in Philipp's words, 'At the Institut, he had been an astonishingly animating force, and never had a Permanent Secretary been so greatly respected.'[39] At the conclusion, Dupré played the Symphonie 'Romane',[40] and afterwards, a little group of Widor's close friends 'waited for him to come down from the organ loft. He came with tears in his eyes, and all embraced in silence.' The coffin was taken to its final resting place in the crypt behind a plain wooden grille; apart from relatives, only Hawkins was permitted to sprinkle holy water on his remains.[41]

The year 1937 also saw the deaths of Vierne, Pierné, Ravel, and Roussel. Widor's long life had witnessed a turbulent span of history, and perhaps we can only be thankful that he did not live to see the impending disaster of 1940 in which the Third Republic was swept away in the torrent of German invasion and occupation. His works remain to remind future generations of the values of civilized life all too easily forgotten in an age of genocide and atomic warfare. The tribute which Edward Gibbon received from Lord Sheffield may also serve for Widor.

Perhaps no man ever divided time more fairly between literary labour and social enjoyment: and hence, probably, he derived his peculiar excellence of making his very extensive knowledge contribute, in the highest degree, to the use or pleasure of those with whom he conversed. He united, in the happiest manner imaginable, two characters which are not always found in the same person, the profound scholar and the peculiarly agreeable companion.[42]

NOTES

Introduction

1. See C. and E. Cavaillé-Coll, *Aristide Cavaillé-Coll: ses origines, sa vie, ses œuvres* (Paris 1929), passim.
2. Zeldin, *France 1848-1945* (Oxford, 1979-81). 'Taste and Corruption', 232-6.
3. Vidler, *The Church in an Age of Revolution* (London 1961), 151.
4. Widor, 'L'Orgue moderne', *Bulletin de l'Académie des Beaux-Arts* (1927), 163.
5. Douglass, *Cavaillé-Coll and the Musicians* (Raleigh, NC, 1980), 106.
6. C. and E. Cavaillé-Coll, *Cavaillé-Coll*, 90-1.
7. Widor, 'L'Orgue moderne', 167.
8. Widor, 'La Classe d'orgue du Conservatoire de Paris', *Le Ménéstrel*, June, 1921.
9. C. and E. Cavaillé-Coll, *Cavaillé-Coll*, 91-2.
10. Widor, 'L'Orgue moderne', 167.
11. C. and E. Cavaillé-Coll, *Cavaillé-Coll*, 96-7.

Chapter 1

1. I am obliged to the Mairie de Lyon for this information.
2. Dumesnil, *Portraits de musiciens français* (Paris, 1938), 197.
3. Article on Widor in *Salut Public* (Lyon newspaper), 17 Mar. 1889.
4. Vallas, *César Franck* (New York, 1951), 65.
5. Douglass, *Cavaillé-Coll and the Musicians* (Raleigh, NC, 1980), 363.
6. Feuillerat, *Paul Bourget* (Paris, 1937), 399.
7. Rostaing, *La Famille Montgolfier* (Lyon, 1910), 108-12.
8. I am indebted to M. Charles Jaillet for this information.
9. Dickens, *Pictures from Italy* (London, 1844; repr. 1967), 321.
10. *Salut Public*, 17 Mar. 1889.
11. Imbert, *Portraits et études* (Paris, 1894), 38.
12. *Salut Public*, 17 Mar. 1889.
13. C. and E. Cavaillé-Coll, *Aristide Cavaillé-Coll; ses origines, sa vie, ses œuvres* (Paris, 1929), 154.
14. Article in *Monde Judiciare*, 4 Apr. 1892.

15. Dupré, 'Souvenirs sur Ch.-M. Widor', *Bulletin de l'Académie des Beaux-Arts* (1959), 28.
16. The exact dates of Widor's time in Brussels can only be surmised, since no record exists at the Brussels Conservatoire; nor is the date of his Baccalauréat recorded at the Académie de Lyon. As Dupré tells us ('Souvenirs', 29), Widor was in Brussels for four years at some point after 1858; Widor is quoted by Vierne (*Mes Souvenirs* (Paris, 1939), 36) as being with Lemmens at the age of 20. In Sept. 1865 he was in Portugal. Therefore his studies probably took place from Feb. 1861 to May 1864.
17. Widor, 'L'Orgue moderne', *Bulletin de l'Académie des Beaux-Arts* (1927), 168.
18. Wagner, *Mein Leben* (Eng. trans., Cambridge, 1983), 611.
19. Widor, Introduction to A. Pirro: *Johann Sébastien Bach* (Paris, 1902).

Chapter 2

1. Fétis, supplement to *Biographie universelle des musiciens* (Paris, 1878-80), 669.
2. Boschot, *Notice sur la vie et l'œuvre de Widor* (Paris, 1937).
3. C. and E. Cavaillé-Coll, *Aristide Cavaillé-Coll; ses origines, sa vie, ses œuvres* (Paris, 1929), 105-6, 115.
4. *Jornal de Noticias* (Oporto), Sept. 1865.
5. The dates of publication of both the Opp. 13 and 42 sets of organ symphonies have been finally established by John Richard Near; see his 'The Life and Work of Charles-Marie Widor', (Doctoral thesis, University of Boston, 1985).
6. Dupré, 'Souvenirs sur Ch.-M. Widor', *Bulletin de l'Académie des Beaux-Arts* (1959), 30.
7. Imbert, *Portraits et études* (Paris, 1894), 38.
8. Vierne, *Mes Souvenirs* (Paris, 1939), 50.
9. Widor, *Académie des Beaux-Arts: fondations, portraits de Massenet à Paladilhe* (Paris, 1927), 160.
10. See Smith, *Alkan: The Enigma* (London, 1976), and Widor, 'L'Orgue moderne', *Bulletin de l'Académie des Beaux-Arts* (1927) for Widor's view that Alkan's compositions are 'today very unjustly neglected'.
11. Widor, 'Le plainchant de Solesmes' (1904), unpublished MS in the Archives de la Maison Diocésaine, Paris.
12. Widor, *Technique de l'orchestre moderne* (Eng. rev. trans., 1946), 146.
13. Widor, MS memorandum (1927), Archives de l'Institut de France.

14. Wagner, *Mein Leben* (Eng. trans., Cambridge, 1983), 623.
15. d'Erlanger, *Quelques souvenirs de France* (privately printed, 1978), 8-48.
16. C. and E. Cavaillé-Coll, *Cavaillé-Coll*, 101-4.
17. Boschot, *Notice sur la vie et l'œuvre de Widor*.
18. Vallas, *César Franck* (New York, 1951), 125, and Smith, *Toward an Authentic Interpretation of the Organ Works of César Franck* (New York, 1983), 149.
19. Dupré, 'Souvenirs', 29; and *Excelsior* (Paris newspaper), 3 Apr. 1934.

Chapter 3

1. Dupré, 'Souvenirs sur Ch.-M. Widor', *Bulletin de l'Académie des Beaux-Arts* (1959), 29.
2. Dupré, *Marcel Dupré raconte* (Paris, 1972), 62.
3. Hamel, *Historie de l'église de Saint-Sulpice* (Paris, 1900), 486.
4. Dupré, *Marcel Dupré raconte*, 62.
5. Gibbon, *Memoirs of my Life* (new edn., London, 1984), 135.
6. Hamel, *Histoire*, 83.
7. Hamel, *Histoire*, 373, 380.
8. C. and E. Cavaillé-Coll, *Aristide Cavaillé-Coll; ses origines, sa vie, ses œuvres* (Paris, 1929), 87-9.
9. Hamel, *Histoire*, 382.
10. Widor to Marie Trélat, 31 July 1896, in Bib. Nat.; see also article on Widor in *Journal* (Paris newspaper), 10 Apr. 1934.
11. Fontoulieu, *Les Eglises de Paris sous la Commune* (Paris, 1873), 247-50.
12. *Journal*, 10 Apr. 1934.
13. Dumesnil, *Portraits de musiciens français* (Paris, 1938), 198.
14. C. and E. Cavaillé-Coll, *Cavaillé-Coll*, 146.
15. Stiven, *In the Organ Lofts of Paris* (Boston, 1923), 57, and information given to me by Mrs Ann Maddocks. Unfortunately there are no references to Widor in the Royal engagements diaries at Windsor.
16. Dupré, 'Souvenirs', 31.
17. Vierne, *Mes Souvenirs* (Paris, 1939), 43.
18. d'Erlanger, *Quelques souvenirs de France* (privately printed, 1978), 48.
19. Landormy, *La Musique française de Franck à Debussy* (Paris, 1943), 170-2.
20. Stiven, *In the Organ Lofts of Paris*, 58-9.
21. Hamel, *Histoire*, 480.

22. Jullian, *Robert de Montesquiou, un Prince 1900* (Paris, 1965), 108.
23. Blanche, *La Pêche aux souvenirs* (Paris, 1949), 145.
24. See Near, 'The Life and Work of Charles-Marie Widor' (Doctoral thesis, University of Boston, 1985) for the dating of the organ symphonies.
25. For a discussion of Symphonies Nos. 7 and 8, see Chapter 5 below.
26. Hamel, *Histoire*, 397, 406-8.
27. Gavoty, *Louis Vierne: La vie et l'œuvre* (Paris, 1943), 55.
28. Widor, Introduction to André Pirro: *Johann Sébastien Bach* (Paris, 1902).
29. Vierne, *Mes Souvenirs* 31-2.
30. Philipp, 'Charles-Marie Widor, a Portrait', *Musical Quarterly*, 30 (1944), 130-1.

Chapter 4

1. Philipp, 'Charles-Marie Widor, a Portrait', *Musical Quarterly*, 30 (1944), 125-6.
2. Imbert, *Portraits et études* (Paris, 1894), 31-2
3. Landormy, *La Musique française de Franck à Debussy* (Paris, 1943), 170-2.
4. Imbert, *Portraits*, 33-4.
5. Varèse, *Edgar Varèse; A Looking-Glass Diary* (London, 1973), 42.
6. Vierne, *Mes Souvenirs* (Paris, 1939), 28.
7. Imbert, *Portraits*, 35-6.
8. Zeldin, *France 1848-1945*, (Oxford, 1979-81), 'Politics and Anger', 321; 'Taste and Corruption', 245.
9. Zeldin, *France*, 'Anxiety and Hypocrisy', 45-8.
10. Imbert, *Portraits*, 37.
11. Zeldin, *France*, 'Politics and Anger', 283.
12. Reclus, *Jules Ferry* (Paris, 1947).
13. Philipp, 'Widor', 129.
14. I am indebted to Dr W. G. Ibberson for this information.
15. Berlioz, *Mémoires* (Eng. trans., New York, 1966), 204-5, 208, 216.
16. Bellanger, *Histoire générale de la presse française* (Paris, 1969), 208-9.
17. Widor, *Académie des Beaux-Arts: fondations, portraits de Massenet à Paladilhe* (Paris, 1927), 177-8.
18. Reclus, *Ferry*.
19. Reclus, *Ferry*, 202-3.
20. Reclus, *Ferry*, 411, and Bellanger, *Histoire*, 203, 361.
21. Widor to Marie Trélat, Sept. 1892, Bib. Nat.

22. *Le Ménéstrel*, Feb. 1882.
23. Proust, *A la recherche du temps perdu* (Paris 1913-27), 'Le Côté de Guermantes', 430.
24. Magnus, *King Edward the Seventh* (London, 1964), 130-1.
25. de Noailles, *Le Livre de ma vie* (Paris, 1932), 13-14.
26. Zamoyski, *Paderewski* (London, 1982), 47-9.
27. *Le Ménéstrel*, June 1882.
28. E. Lamy to Widor, 27 Dec. 1883, Archives de l'Institut de France.
29. Painter, *Marcel Proust* (London, 1959), 166.
30. Blanche, *La Pêche aux souvenirs* (Paris, 1949), 163, 172.
31. Montesquiou, *Les Pas effacés* (Paris, 1923), 51-2.
32. Proust, *Chroniques* (Paris, 1927), 58.
33. Bourget to Widor, 30 Sept. 1889, Archives de l'Institut de France.
34. de Cossart, *The Food of Love: Princesse Edmond de Polignac (1865-1943) and her Salon* (London, 1978), 31-3.
35. Orledge, *Gabriel Fauré* (London, 1979), 270.
36. Street, *Where Paris Dines* (London, 1929), 30.
37. Philipp, 'Widor', 129-30.
38. Young, ed., *Peter Ilyich Tchaikovsky: Letters to his Family* (London, 1981), 395.
39. Vierne, *Mes Souvenirs*, 118.

Chapter 5

1. Philipp, 'Charles-Marie Widor, a Portrait', *Musical Quarterly*, 30 (1944), 126-7.
2. Vallas, *César Franck* (New York, 1951), 259.
3. d'Erlanger, *Quelques souvenirs de France* (privately printed, 1978), 8-48.
4. *L'Intransigent* (Paris newspaper), 29 Aug. 1933.
5. Dupré, 'Souvenirs sur Ch.-M. Widor', *Bulletin de l'Académie des Beaux-Arts*, (1959), 30.
6. Widor to Marie Trélat, 6-9 Dec. 1882, Bib. Nat.
7. *La Revue musicale*, Jan. 1880.
8. Dupré, 'Souvenirs', 31.
9. *The Letters of Franz Liszt to Olga von Meyendorff*, ed. Waters (Washington DC, 1979), 368, 371.
10. C. and E. Cavaillé-Coll, *Aristide Cavaillé-Coll: ses origines, sa vie, ses œuvres* (Paris, 1929), 116.
11. *Le Ménéstrel*, Sept. 1889.
12. Philipp, 'Widor', 126.
13. d'Erlanger, *Quelques souvenirs de France*, 48.
14. Stiven, *In the Organ Lofts of Paris* (Boston, 1923), 60-1.

15. Widor, 'La Classe d'orgue du Conservatoire de Paris', *Le Ménéstrel*, June 1921.
16. Philipp, 'Widor', 127.
17. de Lescure, *François Coppée* (Paris, 1889), 294.
18. *Le Ménéstrel*, May 1886.
19. Imbert, *Portraits et études* (Paris, 1894), 70-3.
20. Joy, *Music in the Life of Albert Schweitzer* (London, 1953), 44.
21. *Le Ménéstrel*, May 1882.
22. *Le Ménéstrel*, Jan. 1886.
23. Lesure, *Claude Debussy: textes et documents inédites* (Paris, 1962), 98-9.
24. Orledge, *Gabriel Fauré* (London, 1979), 282-3.
25. Joachim to Widor, 12 Mar. 1888, Archives de l'Institut de France.
26. *Le Ménéstrel*, May 1888.
27. Joy, *Schweitzer*, 44.
28. *Musical Times*, 28 (1887), 215.
29. Shaw, *Music in London* (London, 1932-7), 491.
30. Philipp, 'Widor', 131.
31. Widor to Berger, 28 Nov. 1887, British Library (Loan MS 48 (13/36 fos. 1-31).
32. Widor to Berger, 12 Dec. 1887.
33. Widor to Berger, 10 Apr. 1888.
34. Widor to Berger, 10 Apr. 1888.
35. *Musical Times*, 29 (1888), 278-9.
36. *Le Ménéstrel*, Feb. 1880.
37. *Musical Times*, 29 (1888), 278-9.
38. Widor to Berger, 20 Apr. 1888, British Library.
39. Elkin, *Royal Philharmonic* (London, 1946), 84.
40. Philipp, 'Widor', 125, 127.
41. Widor to Berger, 21 Jan. 1890, British Library.
42. *Musical Times* 31 (1890), 212-13.
43. Philipp, 'Widor', 127.
44. *Musical Times* 31 (1890), 212-13.
45. Widor probably to Dorchain (no date or addressee), Brussels Conservatoire.
46. *Le Ménéstrel*, June 1890.
47. *Le Ménéstrel*, June 1890 (published letter from Widor to the conductor, M. G. Wittmann).
48. Imbert, *Portraits*, 34.
49. *Le Ménéstrel*, Oct. 1890.

Chapter 6

1 . Tournemire, *César Franck* (Paris, 1931), 74-5.
2. Tournemire, *César Franck*, 28.

3. Vierne, *Mes Souvenirs* (Paris, 1939), 14-18.
4. Vallas, *César Franck* (New York, 1951), 259.
5. Tournemire, *César Franck*, 71.
6. Vierne, *Mes Souvenirs*, 28.
7. Vallas, *César Franck*, 259.
8. Widor, *Académie des Beaux-Arts: fondations, portraits de Massenet à Paladilhe* (Paris, 1927), 36, and Macfarren, *Memories* (London, 1905), 220.
9. Vierne, *Journal* (Paris, 1970), 166.
10. Widor, 'La Classe d'orgue du Conservatoire de Paris', *Le Ménéstrel*, June 1921.
11. Widor to an unspecified person at the Paris Conservatoire, Nov. 1890, Bib. Nat.
12. Vierne, *Mes Souvenirs*, 29.
13. Widor, Introduction to A. Pirro. *Johann Sébastian Bach* (Paris, 1902).
14. Vierne, *Mes Souvenirs*, 33-9.
15. Widor, Introduction to Pirro: *Bach*.
16. Widor, Introduction to Pirro: *Bach*.
17. Vierne, *Mes Souvenirs*, 36.
18. Article in *Excelsior* (Paris newspaper), 3 Apr. 1934.
19. Widor, article in *Aeolian Review*, March 1899.
20. Vierne, *Journal*, 164-5.
21. Vierne, *Journal*, 165.
22. Tournemire, 'Avec Louis Vierne à la classe d'orgue du Conservatoire de Paris' (Paris, 1939), 128-31.
23. Supplied by the records of the Paris Conservatoire.
24. Vierne, *Mes Souvenirs*, 42.
25. Fauquet, *Catalogue de l'œuvre de Charles Tournemire* (Geneva, 1979).
26. Tournemire, *César Franck*, 70.
27. Vierne, *Mes Souvenirs*, 41.
28. Vierne, *Mes Souvenirs*, 42.
29. Vierne, *Mes Souvenirs*, 44-5.
30. Vierne, *Journal*, 166-7. Dubois, not Thomas, is listed as chairman in the Conservatoire records.
31. Vierne, *Journal*, 166-7.
32. Supplied by Archives Nationales, AJ 37252* 2e registre.
33. Philipp, 'Charles-Marie Widor, a Portrait', *Musical Quarterly*, 30 (1944), 127.
34. Article in *Salut Public* (Lyon newspaper), 5 Aug. 1892.
35. Widor to Marie Trélat, Sept. 1892, Bib. Nat.
36. Widor to Marie Trélat, Jan. 1893, Bib. Nat.
37. Vierne, *Journal*, 165, 167-8.

38. Tournemire to Felix Aprahamian, 28 Mar. 1934: 'A simple remark: I am not a pupil of V. d'Indy. That is a mistake, false information. I don't much like this very cold musician!'
39. Vierne, *Journal*, 168. Thomas, not Dubois, is listed as chairman in the Conservatoire records.
40. Vierne, *Mes Souvenirs*, 49.
41. Nichols, *Ravel* (London, 1977), 33.
42. Vierne, *Journal*, 171-2.

Chapter 7

1. Vierne, *Mes Souvenirs* (Paris, 1939), 119.
2. Widor to Hughes Imbert, 4 Nov. 1894, Bib. Nat.
3. Robert, *La Musique à Paris 1896-7* (Paris, 1898), 170.
4. Widor, 'La Classe d'orgue du Conservatoire de Paris', *Le Ménéstrel*, June 1921.
5. Nectoux, *Gabriel Fauré: Correspondance* (Paris, 1980), 221.
6. Vierne, *Journal* (Paris, 1970), 174.
7. Vierne, *Mes Souvenirs*, 51.
8. Calvocoressi, *Musicians' Gallery* (London, 1933), 19.
9. Calvocoressi, *Musicians' Gallery*, 19.
10 Vierne, *Mes Souvenirs*, 51.
11. Dupré, 'Souvenirs sur Ch.-M. Widor', *Bulletin de l'Académie des Beaux-Arts*, (1959), 32.
12. Widor, *Académie des Beaux-Arts: fondations, portraits de Massenet à Paladilhe* (Paris, 1927), 178-9.
13. Joy, *Music in the Life of Albert Schweitzer* (London, 1953), 147.
14. Jules Ferry to Widor (date unclear, *c.*1890), Archives de l'Institut de France.
15. Joy, *Schweitzer*, 147.
16. C. and E. Cavaillé-Coll, *Aristide Cavaillé-Coll: ses origines, sa vie, ses œuvres* (Paris, 1929), 146.
17. Vierne, *Mes Souvenirs*, 87-8.
18. Vierne, *Mes Souvenirs*, 92-3.
19. Craft, 'Stravinsky in Basle', *Musical Times*, 125 (1984), 644; and Nichols, *Ravel* (London, 1977), 153-4.
20. Philipp, 'Charles-Marie Widor, a Portrait', *Musical Quarterly*, 30 (1944), 127.
21. Maurat, *Souvenirs musicaux et littéraires* (St Etienne, 1977), 81.
22. Myers, *Ravel* (London, 1960), 122.
23. Nichols, *Ravel*, 66-7.
24. *Musical Times*, 50 (1909), 388.
25. Suckling, *Gabriel Fauré* (London, 1946), 21, 31.
26. Supplied by Archives Nationales, AJ37* 138, AJ37* 397.

27. Milhaud, *Notes without Music* (London, 1952), 42.
28. Varèse, *Edgar Varèse: A Looking-Glass Diary* (London, 1973), 41-2, and Archives Nationales, AJ 37 396* and 129*.
29. Rosenstiel, *Nadia Boulanger* (New York, 1982), 62-9.
30. Dupré, *Marcel Dupré raconte* (Paris, 1972), 84.
31. Philipp, 'Widor', 128
32. Gavoty, *Louis Vierne: la vie et l'œuvre* (Paris, 1943), 108.
33. Vierne, *Mes Souvenirs*, 48.

Chapter 8

1. Zeldin, *France 1848-1945* (Oxford, 1979-81), 'Politics and Anger', 283-4.
2. Marty, *L'Action française* (Paris, 1968), 58-61.
3. Joy, *Music in the Life of Albert Schweitzer* (London, 1953), 164-5, and Vierne, *Mes Souvenirs* (Paris, 1939), 96.
4. Barrès, *La Grande Pitié des églises de France* (Paris, 1914), 72-4.
5. Zeldin, *France*, 'Anxiety and Hypocrisy', 45-8.
6. Article in *Excelsior* (Paris newspaper), 3 Apr. 1934.
7. Dupré, 'Souvenirs sur Ch.-M. Widor', *Bulletin de l'Académie des Beaux-Arts* (1959), 27.
8. Vierne, *Mes Souvenirs*, 116.
9. Joy, *Schweitzer*, 163.
10. Widor, *Académie des Beaux-Arts: fondations, portraits de Massenet à Paladilhe* (Paris, 1927), 228.
11. Widor, 'Le plainchant de Solesmes' (1904), unpublished MS in the Archives de la Maison Diocésaine, Paris.
12. Saint-Saëns, *Ecole buissonnière* (Paris, 1913), 180, and d'Indy, *La Schola Cantorum en 1925* (Paris, 1927), 30.
13. Widor, *Initiation musicale* (Paris, 1923), 107.
14. C. and E. Cavaillé-Coll, *Aristide Cavaillé-Coll: ses origines, sa vie, ses œuvres* (Paris, 1929), 133-6.
15. Hollins, *A Blind Musician Looks Back* (London, 1936), 233.
16. I am indebted to Dr W. G. Ibberson for this information.
17. I am indebted to Mrs Ann Maddocks for this information.
18. Widor, Introduction to Schweitzer: *J. S. Bach* (London, 1911).
19. Vidler, *The Church in an Age of Revolution* (London, 1961), 182-5.
20. I am indebted to Mrs Ann Maddocks for this information; see also Dupré, *Marcel Dupré raconte* (Paris, 1972), 71.
21. Joy, *Schweitzer*, 43.
22. Munch, *I am a Conductor* (New York, 1955), 15-17.
23. Philipp, 'Charles-Marie Widor, a Portrait', *Musical Quarterly*, 30 (1944), 131.

24. Joy, *Schweitzer*, 157-8, 163.
25. Dupré, *Marcel Dupré raconte*, 71.
26. Joy, *Schweitzer*, 170.
28. Schweitzer, *My Life and Thought* (London, 1931), 154-61.
28. Schweitzer, *My Life and Thought*, 161-2.
29. Widor, Introduction to Schweitzer's *J. S. Bach*.

Chapter 9

1. Dent, *Ferruccio Busoni* (London, 1974), 197; and Dupré, *Marcel Dupré raconte* (Paris, 1972), 150-1.
2. Philipp, 'Charles-Marie Widor, a Portrait', *Musical Quarterly*, 30 (1944), 129.
3. Saint-Saëns to Widor, July 1914, Archives de l'Institut de France.
4. Widor, *Académie des Beaux-Arts: fondations, portraits de Massenet à Paladilhe* (Paris, 1927), 174.
5. Widor, 'Note sur les faits intéressants en 1914', Archives de l'Institut de France.
6. Widor, *Académie*, 174-5.
7. Widor, 'Note'.
8. Widor, *Académie*, 175.
9. Philipp, 'Widor', 132.
10. Philipp, 'Widor', 128.
11. Joy, *Music in the Life of Albert Schweitzer* (London, 1953), 179.
12. Widor, *Académie*, 6-8.
13. Nectoux: *Camille Saint-Saëns et Gabriel Fauré: Correspondance, soixante ans d'amitié* (Paris, 1973), 107-8.
14. Widor, *Académie*, 176.
15. Widor, MS memorandum, Archives de l'Institut de France, and Philipp, 'Widor', 130.
16. Widor, *Académie*, 21-2.
17. Churchill, *Great Contemporaries* (London, 1937), 212.
18. Widor, *Académie*, 22-3.
19. Widor, *Académie*, 101.
20. Boschot, *Notice sur la vie et l'œuvre de Widor* (Paris, 1937).
21. Widor, *Académie*, 23-4.
22. Widor, *Académie*, 30-2.
23. *Musical Times*, 60 (1919).
24. Elgar, 'Mem. l'Institut de Fr.' 19 June 1920. In Hereford and Worcs. County Record Office, 705.445.5016. I am indebted to Jerrold Northrop Moore for this information.
25. Widor, *Académie*, 32-3.
26. Recorded on Widor's birth certificate, Mairie de Lyon.

27. Magnus, *King Edward the Seventh* (London, 1964), 131.
28. Albaret, *Monsieur Proust* (Eng. trans., London., 1973), 241-2. In this account by Proust's housekeeper, Widor's house is wrongly stated as being in the rue La Pérouse.
29. Widor, *Académie*, 247-50.
30. Rosenstiel, *Nadia Boulanger* (New York, 1982), 153-7.
31. Copland, *1900 through 1942* (New York, 1984), 52.
32. Rosenstiel, *Boulanger*, 153-7.
33. Barlow, *Bergson* (Paris, 1966), 84.
34. Widor, *Académie*, 24-7.
35. Philipp, 'Widor', 130.

Chapter 10

1. Widor to Brusel, 30 June 1922, Bib. Nat.
2. Quoted in Rowse, *A Cornishman at Oxford* (London, 1965; repr. 1983), 287.
3. Dumesnil, *La Musique en France entre les deux guerres* (Paris, 1946), 137.
4. Widor, *Académie des Beaux-Arts: fondations, portraits de Massenet à Paladilhe* (Paris, 1927), 194-5.
5. Philipp, 'Charles-Marie Widor, a Portrait', *Musical Quarterly*, 30 (1944), 130.
6. I am indebted to Mrs Ann Maddocks for this information.
7. Widor to Hawkins, 13 Mar. 1927. I am indebted to Mrs Ann Bastow (née Hawkins) for this information.
8. I am indebted to Felix Aprahamian for this information.
9. Dupré, *Marcel Dupré raconte* (Paris, 1972), 117-18; Gavoty, *Louis Vierne: la vie et l'œuvre* (Paris, 1943), 145.
10. I am indebted to Mme Jacqueline Englert-Marchal for this information.
11. Philipp, 'Widor', 129.
12. I am indebted to the late Mme Yvonne Lefébure for this information.
13. Mari, *Messiaen* (Paris, 1965), 13, 15-16.
14. Maximovich to Widor, 9 Feb. 1930, Archives de l'Institut de France.
15. de Beauvoir, *Memoirs of a Dutiful Daughter* (Eng. trans., London, 1963), 132, 135.
16. I am indebted to Felix Aprahamian for this information.
17. *Le Figaro*, 19 and 20 Jan. 1930.
18. I am indebted to Mrs Ann Maddocks for this information; see also Dupré, *Marcel Dupré raconte*, 91.

19. *The Hurst Johnian*, (1931), 313-14.
20. Coppola, *Dix-sept ans de musique à Paris 1922-1939* (Lausanne, 1944; Paris, Geneva, and Slatkine, 1982), 144-7.
21. Vierne, *Mes Souvenirs* (Paris, 1939), 108-9.
22. Dupré, 'Souvenirs sur Ch.-M. Widor', *Bulletin de l'Académie des Beaux-Arts* (1959), 33.
23. Dupré, *Marcel Dupré raconte*, 69-70.
24. Widor to Dukas, 1934, Archives de l'Institut de France.
25. Philipp, 'Widor', 129.
26. Philipp, 'Widor', 131.
27. Dupré, 'Souvenirs', 33.
28. Quoted in Grierson, *Donald Francis Tovey* (London, 1952), 285.
29. Dupré, 'Souvenirs', 33.
30. *Les Débats* (Paris newspaper), 17 Mar. 1937.
31. Dupré, 'Souvenirs', 33.
32. Philipp, 'Widor', 132.
33. Craft, *Stravinsky: Selected Correspondence*, Vol. 2 (London, 1984), 483.
34. *The Hurst Johnian*, (1936), 235-8.
35. Boschot, *Notice sur la vie et l'œuvre de Widor* (Paris, 1937).
36. Dupré, *Marcel Dupré raconte*, 70.
37. Dumesnil, *Portraits de musiciens français* (Paris, 1938), 201-2.
38. Boschot, *Notice sur la vie et l'œuvre de Widor*.
39. Philipp, 'Widor', 132.
40. Dumesnil, *Portraits*, 201-2.
41. I am indebted to Mrs Ann Maddocks for this information.
42. Gibbon, *Memoirs of my Life* (London 1796; new edn. 1984), 192-3.

APPENDIX
CATALOGUE OF WORKS

This Appendix lists the main works of Widor. For a complete list the reader is referred to that provided by John Richard Near in 'The Life and Work of Charles-Marie Widor'.

Chamber

Piano Quintet No. 1, Op. 7, 1868
Piano Trio, Op. 19, 1874
Violin Sonata No. 1, Op. 50, 1881
Piano Quartet, Op. 66, 1891
Piano Quintet No. 2, Op. 68, 1894
Violin Sonata No. 2, Op. 79, 1907
Cello Sonata, Op. 80, 1907

Choral

Deux motets, Op. 18, 1874
Trois motets, Op. 23, 1875
Messe, Op. 36, 1878
Psaume CXII, 1879
Ave Verum Corpus, *c*.1930

Orchestral

Grande Phantasia for organ and orchestra, 1865
Symphonie No. 1, Op. 16, 1873
Piano Concerto No. 1, Op. 39, 1876
Violin Concerto, 1877
Cello Concerto, Op. 41, 1878
Symphonie No. 2, Op. 54, 1882
'La Nuit de Walpurgis', Op. 60, 1888
Fantaisie for Piano and Orchestra, Op. 62, 1889
Symphonie No. 3 for Organ and Orchestra, Op. 69, 1894
Piano Concerto No. 2, Op. 77, 1905
Sinfonia Sacra for Organ and Orchestra, Op. 81, 1907
Symphonie Antique for Chorus and Orchestra, 1911

Organ solo

Symphonies Nos. 1-4, Op. 13, 1872
Symphonies Nos. 5-8, Op. 42, 1887
Symphonie 'Gothique', Op. 70, 1894
Symphonie 'Romane', Op. 73, 1900
Suite Latine, Op. 86, 1927
Trois nouvelles pièces, Op. 87, 1934

Piano solo

Suite, Op. 58, 1887

Songs

Six mélodies, Op. 14, 1872
Six mélodies, Op. 22, 1875
Trois mélodies, Op. 28, 1876
Deux duos, Op. 30, 1876
Trois mélodies italiennes, Op. 32, 1876
Trois mélodies italiennes, Op. 35, 1878
Six mélodies, Op. 37, *c.*1877
Deux duos, Op. 40, 1876
Six mélodies, Op. 43, 1878
Six mélodies, Op. 47, 1879
Deux duos, Op. 52, 1881
Six mélodies, Op. 53, 1881
Soirs d'été, Op. 63, *c.*1889

Stage

La Korrigane, ballet, 1880
Conte d'avril, incidental music, 1885
Les Jacobites, incidental music, 1885
Maître Ambros, drame lyrique, 1886
Jeanne d'Arc, ballet-pantomime, 1890
Les Pêcheurs de Saint-Jean, drame lyrique, 1905
Nerto, drame lyrique, 1924

BIBLIOGRAPHY

Alain, Marie-Claire: Record notes for Erato STU71165 (1980), Widor Organ Symphonies, Nos. 4, 6, 9, and part of No. 3.

Albaret, Celeste: *Monsieur Proust* (Paris, 1973; Eng. trans., London, 1973).

Aprahamian, Felix: Record notes for RCA RL25033 (1976), Widor Organ Symphonies Nos. 1-5.

Barlow, Michel: *Bergson* (Paris, 1966).

Barrès, Maurice: *La Grande Pitié des églises de France* (Paris, 1914).

de Beauvoir, Simone: *Mémoires d'une jeune fille rangée* (Paris, 1958; Eng. trans. *Memoirs of a Dutiful Daughter*, London, 1963).

Bellanger, C.: *Histoire générale de la presse française* (Paris, 1969).

Berlioz, Hector: *Mémoires* (Paris, 1870; Eng. trans., New York, 1966).

Blanche, Jacques-Emile: *La Pêche aux souvenirs* (Paris, 1949).

Boschot, A.: *Notice sur la vie et l'œuvre de Widor* (Paris, 1937).

Calvocoressi, M. D.: *Musicians' Gallery* (London, 1933).

Cavaillé-Coll, C. and E.: *Aristide Cavaillé-Coll: ses origines, sa vie, ses œuvres* (Paris, 1929).

Churchill, Winston: *Great Contemporaries* (London, 1937).

Copland, Aaron: *1900 through 1942* (New York, 1984)

Coppola, Pietro: *Dix-sept ans de musique à Paris 1922-1939* (Lausanne, 1944; Paris, Geneva, and Slatkine, 1982).

de Cossart, Michael: *The Food of Love: Princesse Edmond de Polignac (1865-1943) and her Salon* (London, 1978).

Craft, Robert, ed: *Stravinsky: Selected Correspondence*, vol. 2 (London, 1984).

—— 'Stravinsky in Basle', *Musical Times*, 125 (1984), 644.

Dent, E. J.: *Ferruccio Busoni* (London, 1974).

Dickens, Charles: *Pictures from Italy* (London, 1844; repr. 1967).

Douglass, Fenner: *Cavaillé-Coll and the Musicians* (Raleigh, NC, 1980).

Dumesnil, R.: *Portraits de musiciens français* (Paris, 1938).

—— *La Musique en France entre les deux guerres* (Paris, 1946).

Dupré, Marcel: 'Souvenirs sur Ch.-M. Widor', *Bulletin de l'Académie des Beaux-Arts* (1959).

—— *Marcel Dupré raconte* (Paris, 1972).

Elkin, Robert: *Royal Philharmonic* (London, 1946).

d'Erlanger, E. B.: *Quelques souvenirs de France* (privately printed, 1978).

Fauquet, J.-M.: *Catalogue de l'œuvre de Charles Tournemire* (Geneva, 1979).

Fétis, François Joseph: *Biographie universelle des musiciens* (Brussels, 1835-44; supplement added by A. Pougin, Paris, 1878-80).

Feuillerat, A.: *Paul Bourget* (Paris, 1937).

Fontoulieu, V. P.: *Les Eglises de Paris sous la Commune* (Paris, 1873).

Gavoty, Bernard: *Louis Vierne: la vie et l'œuvre* (Paris, 1943).

Gibbon, Edward: *Memoirs of my Life* (London, 1796; new edn. 1984).

Grierson, Mary: *Donald Francis Tovey* (London, 1952).

Hamel, G.: *Histoire de l'église de Saint-Sulpice* (Paris, 1900).

Hollins, Alfred: *A Blind Musician Looks Back* (London, 1936).

Imbert, H.: *Portraits et études* (Paris, 1894).

d'Indy, Vincent: *La Schola Cantorum en 1925* (Paris, 1927).

Joy, C. R.: *Music in the Life of Albert Schweitzer* (London, 1953).

Jullian, Philippe: *Robert de Montesquiou, un Prince 1900* (Paris, 1965).

Landormy, P.: *La Musique française de Franck à Debussy* (Paris, 1943).

de Lescure, M.: *François Coppée* (Paris, 1889).

Lesure, F.: *Claude Debussy: textes et documents inédites* (Paris, 1962).

Macfarren, Walter: *Memories* (London, 1905).

Magnus, Philip: *King Edward the Seventh* (London, 1964).

Mari, Pierrette, *Messiaen* (Paris, 1965).

Marty, A.: *L'Action française* (Paris, 1968).

Maurat, E.: *Souvenirs musicaux et littéraires* (St Etienne, 1977).

Milhaud, Darius: *Notes without Music* (London, 1952).

Montesquiou, Robert de: *Les Pas éffaces* (Paris, 1923).

Munch, Charles: *I am a Conductor* (New York, 1955).

Myers, Rollo H.: *Ravel* (London, 1960).

Near, John Richard: 'The Life and Work of Charles-Marie Widor', (Doctoral thesis, University of Boston, 1985).

Nectoux, J. M., ed.: *Gabriel Fauré: Correspondance* (Paris, 1980).

—— *Camille Saint-Saëns et Gabriel Fauré: Correspondance, soixante ans d'amitié* (Paris, 1973).

Nichols, Roger: *Ravel* (London, 1977).

de Noailles, Anna: *Le Livre de ma vie* (Paris, 1932).

Orledge, Robert: *Gabriel Fauré* (London, 1979).

Painter, George: *Marcel Proust* (London, 1959).

Philipp, Isidor: 'Charles-Marie Widor, a Portrait', *Musical Quarterly*, 30 (1944), 125.

Proust, Marcel: *A la recherche du temps perdu* (Paris, 1913-27).

—— *Chroniques* (Paris, 1927).

Reclus, Maurice: *Jules Ferry* (Paris, 1947).

Robert, G.: *La Musique à Paris 1896-7* (Paris, 1898).

Rosenstiel, Leonie: *Nadia Boulanger* (New York, 1982).

Rostaing, H.: *La Famille Montgolfier* (Lyon, 1910).

Rowse, A. L.: *A Cornishman at Oxford* (London, 1965; repr. 1983).

Saint-Saëns, Camille: *Ecole buissonnière* (Paris, 1913).

Schweitzer, Albert: *My Life and Thought* (London, 1931).

Shaw, George Bernard: *Music in London* (London, 1932-7).

Smith, Rollin: *Toward an Authentic Interpretation of the Organ Works of César Franck* (New York, 1983).

Smith, Ronald: *Alkan, the Enigma* (London, 1976).

Stiven, Frederic B.: *In the Organ Lofts of Paris* (Boston, 1923).

Street, Julian: *Where Paris Dines* (London, 1929).

Suckling, Norman: *Gabriel Fauré* (London, 1946).

Thomson, Andrew: 'C.-M. Widor, a Revaluation', *Musical Times*, 125 (1984), 169.

Tournemire, Charles: *César Franck* (Paris, 1931).

—— 'Avec Louis Vierne à la classe d'orgue du Conservatoire de Paris', in the supplement to Vierne's *Mes Souvenirs* (Paris, 1939).

Vallas, L.: *César Franck* (New York, 1951).

Varèse, Louise: *Edgar Varèse: A Looking-Glass Diary* (London, 1973).

Vidler, Alec R.: *The Church in an Age of Revolution* (London, 1961).

Vierne, Louis: *Mes Souvenirs* (Paris, 1939).

—— *Journal* (Paris, 1970).

Wagner, Richard: *Mein Leben* (published privately, 1870-81; Eng. trans. *My Life*, Cambridge, 1983).

Waters, Edward N., ed.: *The Letters of Franz Liszt to Olga von Meyendorff* (Washington DC, 1979).

Widor, Charles-Marie: Introduction to A. Pirro: *L'Orgue de Jean-Sebastien Bach* (Paris, 1895).

—— Introduction to A. Pirro: *Johann Sébastien Bach* (Paris, 1902).

—— *Technique de l'orchestre moderne* (Paris, 1904; rev., 1925; Eng. trans., 1906; rev., 1946).

—— Introductions to A. Schweitzer: *J. S. Bach* (Paris and Leipzig, 1905; Leipzig, 1908; London, 1911).

—— 'La Classe d'orgue du Conservatoire de Paris', *Le Ménéstrel* June 1921.

—— *Initiation musicale* (Paris, 1923).

—— *Académie des Beaux-Arts: fondations, portraits de Massenet à Paladilhe* (Paris, 1927).

—— 'L'Orgue moderne', *Bulletin de l'Académie des Beaux-Arts* (1927).

Young, Percy M., ed.: *Peter Ilyich Tchaikovsky: Letters to his Family* (London, 1981).

Zamoyski, Adam: *Paderewski* (London, 1982).

Zeldin, Theodore: *France 1848-1945* (Oxford, 1973-7; paperback edn. 1979-81).

INDEX